Y0-BCV-667

CRITICIZING THE MEDIA

The SAGE CommText Series

Series Editor:
EVERETTE E. DENNIS
Gannett Center for Media Studies, Columbia University

Founding Editor: F. GERALD KLINE, *late of the School of Journalism and Mass Communication, University of Minnesota*
Founding Associate Editor: SUSAN H. EVANS, *Annenberg School of Communications, University of Southern California*

The **SAGE CommText** series brings the substance of mass communication scholarship to student audiences by blending syntheses of current research with applied ideas in concise, moderately priced volumes. Designed for use both as supplementary readings and as "modules" with which the teacher can "create" a new text, the **SAGE CommTexts** give students a conceptual map of the field of communication and media research. Some books examine topical areas and issues; others discuss the implications of particular media; still others treat methods and tools used by communication scholars. Written by leading researchers with the student in mind, the **SAGE CommTexts** provide teachers in communication and journalism with solid supplementary materials.

Available in this series:

1. TELEVISION IN AMERICA
   George Comstock
2. COMMUNICATION HISTORY
   John D. Stevens and
   Hazel Dicken Garcia
3. PRIME-TIME TELEVISION:
   Content and Control
   Muriel G. Cantor
4. MOVIES AS MASS COMMUNICATION
   Garth Jowett and James M. Linton
5. CONTENT ANALYSIS: An Introduction
   to Its Methodology
   Klaus Krippendorff
6. INTERPERSONAL COMMUNICATION:
   The Social Exchange Approach
   Michael E. Roloff
7. THE CARTOON:
   Communication to the Quick
   Randall P. Harrison
8. ADVERTISING AND SOCIAL CHANGE
   Ronald Berman
9. COMPARATIVE COMMUNICATION
   RESEARCH
   Alex S. Edelstein
10. MEDIA ANALYSIS TECHNIQUES
    Arthur Asa Berger
11. SHAPING THE FIRST AMENDMENT:
    The Development of Free Expression
    John D. Stevens
12. THE SOAP OPERA
    Muriel G. Cantor and
    Suzanne Pingree

13. THE DISSIDENT PRESS: Alternative
    Journalism in American History
    Lauren Kessler
14. TELEVISION AND CHILDREN: A Special
    Medium for a Special Audience
    Aimée Dorr
15. PRECISION JOURNALISM:
    A Practical Guide
    David Pearce Demers
    and Suzanne Nichols
16. PUBLIC RELATIONS:
    What Research Tells Us
    John V. Pavlik
17. NEW ELECTRONIC PATHWAYS:
    Videotex, Teletext, and
    Online Databases
    Jerome Aumente
18. THE TELEVISION NEWS INTERVIEW
    Akiba A. Cohen
19. UNDERSTANDING VIDEO:
    Applications, Impact, and Theory
    Jarice Hanson
20. EXAMINING NEWSPAPERS:
    What Research Reveals About
    America's Newspapers
    Gerald Stone
21. CRITICIZING THE MEDIA:
    Empirical Approaches
    James B. Lemert

additional titles in preparation

James B. Lemert

CRITICIZING THE MEDIA

Empirical Approaches

LIBRARY
COLBY-SAWYER COLLEGE
NEW LONDON, NH 03257

Volume 21. The Sage COMMTEXT Series

SAGE PUBLICATIONS
The Publishers of Professional Social Science
Newbury Park   London   New Delhi

P
96
.C76
L46
1989

Copyright © 1989 by Sage Publications, Inc.

All rights reserved. No part of this book may be reproduced or utilized
in any form or by any means, electronic or mechanical, including
photocopying, recording, or by any information storage and retrieval
system, without permission in writing from the publisher.

For information address:

SAGE Publications, Inc.
2111 West Hillcrest Drive
Newbury Park, California 91320

SAGE Publications Ltd.
28 Banner Street
London EC1Y 8QE
England

SAGE Publications India Pvt. Ltd.
M-32 Market
Greater Kailash I
New Delhi 110 048 India

Printed in the United States of America

Library of Congress Cataloging-in-Publication Data

Lemert, James B., 1935-
    Criticizing the media : empirical approaches / by James B. Lemert.
        p.   cm. — (Sage commtext series ; v. 21)
    Includes bibliographies and index.
    ISBN 0-8039-2636-7 — ISBN 0-8039-2637-5 (pbk.)
    1. Mass media criticism.   I. Title.   II. Series
P96.C76L46   1989
001.51—dc19   88-32685
                                                                      CIP

First Printing 1989

104892

CONTENTS

Acknowledgments   7

1 Introduction   9

   The Purpose of This Book   11
   The Need for Critics   12
   Conclusions   19
   Notes   20
   References   21

2 The "State of the Art" Among Critics   22

   Institutional Biases   23
   Criticism for Whom?   25
   Divided, We Fail   26
   Summary   32
   Notes   33
   References   33

3 Administrative and Critical Media Research   34

   Administrative Research   38
   Critical Research   39
   What Empirical Criticism Can Do   40
   References   42

4 Tools the Empiricists Use   43

   Variables and Hypotheses   44
   Designing Empirical Studies   47
   Summary   57
   Study Exercises   58
   References   58

**5 The Common Bond: Empirical and
   Social Responsibility Criticisms**   60

   "The Mistress or the Maid?"   60
   Counting Noses (or Whatever)   65
   The "Sins of Sears"   66

Labor in the News   70
A Chicano Strike in Texas   72
"The Same Old Mistakes"   74
Summary   82
References   83

6   Doing Empirical Criticism of Media Performance   85

Effects of Chain Ownership   85
"Afghanistanism" in Environmental News   91
A Critique of Rape Coverage   94
"Whodunit?"   98
The Official Source Syndrome   101
Summary and Overview   105
References   105

7   Systematic Criticism and Media Studies   107

Three False Truisms   107
Criteria for a Critical Tradition   108
Some Ideas for Studies   109
Conclusion   115
References   115

Name Index   116

Subject Index   119

About the Author   122

ACKNOWLEDGMENTS

I would like to thank the professional staff at Sage Publications for their cooperativeness and forbearance—especially Everette E. Dennis, the director of the Gannett Center for Media Studies, Columbia University, and editor of the CommText Series.

University of Oregon colleagues Greg Kerber and Arnold Ismach were an enormous help in critiquing and advising me about the manuscript. They contributed much to any strengths the book may have; I must bear responsibility for any weaknesses, of course.

As always, Rosalie Lemert and her mighty word processor made an indispensable contribution. She also contributed the kind of sharp-eyed, constructive criticism that made it a challenge even to get these imperfect words past her scrutiny and onto the word processor.

—James B. Lemert

1

INTRODUCTION

Critics of the news media lack a sustained tradition, and this lack helps journalists resist needed change.

The American newspapers are the most base, false, servile and venal publications that ever polluted the fountains of society [John Ward Fenno, writing in his *Gazette of the United States,* 1799].

Nothing can now be believed which is seen in a newspaper. Truth itself becomes suspicious by being put into that polluted vehicle [Thomas Jefferson, in a letter to J. Norvell, 1807].

Mankind cannot now be governed without [the press], nor at present with it [John Adams, in a letter to a friend, 1815].

A news writer is one who has failed in his calling [Otto Von Bismarck, speech given November 10, 1862].

You [journalists] who take the fair body of truth and sell it to the marketplace, who betray the virgin hopes of mankind into the loathsome brothel of big business [Upton Sinclair, 1919: 436].

A city with one newspaper . . . is like a man with one eye, and often the eye is glass [A. J. Liebling, 1961: 29].

Quotable critical "zingers" about the news media have been easy to find as long as there have been media purporting to tell us about our world.[1] The above examples date from just after the founding of the Republic to the post-World War II years, when A. J. Liebling of the *New Yorker* was writing a notable chapter in press criticism. And, in some ways at least, what is being written and said today about print and broadcast news media sounds much the same. For instance, in recent years people have applied the following to the news media and/or journalists:

"nattering nabobs of negativism,"

"servants of the status quo,"

"elitist liberal establishment media,"

"ghouls, cowards and creeps who put private grief onto endlessly replayed news videotape,"

"protectors of capitalism," and (just as often),

"radical leftists who have stealthily undermined capitalism."

Yes, zingers and one-liners about the media always have been plentiful. But three other things may well be in short supply.

(1) While there is a very long tradition of complaints and criticism of the news media, this criticism has come from outside the news media more often than from within them. The relatively recent mechanisms of criticism that have been partly rooted *within* the news media—such as news councils, journalism reviews, and the ombudsman movement— have run into deep-seated resistance.

(2) Critics of the news media lack a sustained tradition of reasoned critical analysis. To sling one-liners at the news media may be satisfying, but that's really only a form of name-calling. What form, then, should a reasoned critical analysis take? Journalism professor Lee Brown (1974: 17-20) provides a good outline for such a sustained tradition. According to Brown, criticism of news media performance should be based on *shared standards and values* established ahead of time. These standards and values should be "visible to and known by the public, the critic and those to be criticized." Furthermore, the criticisms themselves should be made *public*—as should be the methodology used to do the analysis and to reach those critical conclusions. Brown argues as well that criticisms should be "*realistic* in that response is possible and guidance [suggestions for improvement] is offered." As Chapter 2 makes clear, no consensus exists—even among critics of the news media—on the values, standards, and procedures to be used in critical analysis. Moreover, some schools of criticism seem remarkably silent regarding guidance toward specific improvements to be made in journalistic practices. Further, it's hard to avoid the impression, at times, that some critical writing is intended to be read within a fairly small circle of like-minded critics. In other words, in some media criticism, the desired characteristics Brown has laid out are missing.

(3) In the last analysis, for criticism to lead journalists and news media management to make constructive changes, media personnel must be willing to make those changes once critical analysis convinces

them that a practice should be changed. Given the disarray and contradictions present among critics, it should be no surprise to find that many journalists may have trouble sorting workable ideas out of a confusing cacophony of critical voices. However, critics aren't the only problem here. As much of the present chapter argues, some working journalists themselves have a record of opposition and resistance to criticism, however constructive.

THE PURPOSE OF THIS BOOK

Not all media criticism comes from media people and their public or private sector detractors. Some of it is generated by the academy—by educators, especially those in media studies, communication, and journalism departments. For too long, some self-described media critics have either ignored or denigrated the insights and contributions available to them in the work of mass communication researchers. This book is intended to show, in specific and practical ways, how much has been missed by ignoring the empirically based literature of criticism, and how *social science techniques* can be used to evaluate and criticize the performance of present and future news media.

Chapter 1 tackles the most basic of questions about critics and criticism: Who are they, and do we need them? Chapter 2 covers some of the reasons much of the critical literature has ignored or downplayed the contributions of mass communication research. Chapter 3 tries to set in context, restate, and clarify a distinction made by scholars more than 40 years ago between "administrative" and "critical" research, and then goes on to suggest five major contributions empirical research can make to media criticism. Chapter 4 provides some insight into why empirical researchers think the way they do when they engage in critical studies, and examines the tools they have at their disposal. These chapters and the remainder of the book (1) give examples of criticisms based on empirical findings, (2) demonstrate that, often, both empirical and other critics are saying similar things and thus can be mutually reinforcing, (3) suggest how to think about doing such research in the future, and (4) suggest some new questions all of us should be asking about the news media.

This book is meant for both persons who have no intention of ever doing empirical research and those who think they might. Doing empirical research to assess news media performance probably isn't as important to journalists and all types of critics as being able to read, appreciate, recognize, and understand criticisms that others have based on empirical findings. The ranks of insightful critics are too thin—and the need for constructive change in news practices too great—for any "school" of criticism to fight for exclusive turf.

My arguments here are not meant to imply that all criticisms of the news media are warranted—or even made with good intentions. Journalists have the same right as anyone else to ask critics for documentation and explanation. One purpose of this book is to demonstrate how empirical researchers document their criticisms of news media practices.

THE NEED FOR CRITICS

Perhaps criticism from outside the field of journalism would be unnecessary if journalists and the news media had shown they could strip off the blinders tradition has placed on them and take a fresh look at themselves.

If self-examination by professional journalists were done, it could take several possible forms. Some of them have been tried, with promising results. However, none has ever been tried often enough, and with such universally praised results, that we can feel secure in the knowledge that journalism is so automatically self-correcting that there's no need for criticism by "outsiders."

The following is a short list of some forms of self-examination by journalists. Most of them will be considered in more detail later.

- *In-house* criticism. These examples of critical comment developed inside news and other media organizations range all the way from daily postings of a thoroughly critiqued newspaper by a senior editor, to "winners and sinners" memos by editors, to weekly staff critique sessions, to informal bull sessions among journalists. As the name implies, these critiques do not reach the public print or airways.
- The *ombudsman.* A part-time or full-time staffer is assigned to investigate complaints or issues raised by audience members. Sometimes, but not always, the results of the investigations are made public through a regular column.
- *Professional societies* of journalists. For example, in Arizona, the Society of Professional Journalists/Sigma Delta Chi chapter did a critical analysis of the role a radio station's newsman played in stimulating street rioting near a university campus. I would include here as well articles and commentary in such professional magazines as *Quill* and *Editor & Publisher.*
- *Journalism reviews.* In the 1960s and early 1970s, many urban centers had at least one such magazine-style review, featuring vigorous, no-holds-barred

criticism by reporters and ex-reporters. Although some of these publications died, others—like the *Washington Journalism Review, Columbia Journalism Review*, and *St. Louis Journalism Review*—thrive. In addition, many urban weeklies, from the *Village Voice* to the *Reader* of Seattle, have regular media review columns.

- *News councils* that have journalists as at least some of their members. News councils receive complaints, investigate them, and invite testimony from journalists and others involved. These should not be confused with community press councils, which are formed from members of the community.
- *Media news/reviews/columns.* The news magazines generally have a section of news about the media in them. People like Jeff Greenfield of ABC News and David Shaw of the *Los Angeles Times* have done similar reporting/commentary for network and newspaper audiences.
- *Reflections and commentary.* Journalists themselves, especially senior, respected ones, comment on what's wrong with journalism as they relate their experiences in autobiographies, retirement speeches, or invited addresses.

Ironically, some distinguished ex-editors, such as Harry Ashmore, have argued that journalists simply aren't capable of effectively criticizing their own practices (cited in Brown, 1974: 16). But if vigorous and searching self-criticism were to occur consistently among practicing journalists, the need for criticism by "outsiders" might go away. Unfortunately, *if* is the biggest little word in the English language.

The Weight of Tradition

Journalism is a very tradition-bound craft. Many of its traditions provide quick and easy solutions to the problem of coping quickly with the flood of editing and writing decisions journalists must make daily. Journalists can be so busy each day editing videotape or writing newspaper copy that they seldom have the time and energy to stop and question what these traditions have permitted them to do. Of course, many newspeople do question craft practices on occasion, but often (a) it is after, not before or during, their use of habitual formulae, (b) those thoughts aren't communicated to anyone in a position to do something constructive about them, and (c) too soon, it's time to start on another story. Furthermore, if such questions keep recurring, the journalist's "efficiency" (as the newsroom defines it) may be called into question.

Journalistic traditions weigh heavily for many other reasons besides the fact that many journalists are too busy using these traditions to think much about them. As many writers have pointed out, a sense of service to the public is a major reason talented women and men are attracted to journalism, and a major reason many of them stay, in spite of mixed support from the public and often modest pay (see, e.g., Edelstein, 1966; Lemert, 1970). Especially in the absence of other sources of recognition[2] and reward, journalists' job-related sense of worth can depend on their belief that they are rendering a public service. Imagine, then, how threatening it can be if somebody comes along and says, in effect, that these journalists have been doing the public a disservice throughout their professional lives. No wonder, then, that some journalists are notorious for defensiveness in the face of actual—or even potential—criticism of what they are very much in the habit of doing.

When that criticism comes from outside the craft, many journalists' first response will be that the critic just "doesn't know the business," and therefore can be ignored. Notice the change of subject here. Instead of talking about the criticism, we are now talking about the critic, and it's the journalist who seems to be in charge of deciding who is eligible to be a critic.

Finally, notice that the journalist who dismisses criticisms by "outsiders" because they couldn't possibly be knowledgeable may very well turn right around and claim that any good "general assignment" reporter can readily understand everybody else's business.

When the criticism comes instead from *inside* the newsroom—perhaps from a newspaper's ombudsman—it can make editors and reporters "insecure and paranoid" (Mogavero, 1982). (More about the ombudsman shortly.)

Journalists' defensiveness can help produce the "glass house syndrome" that many journalists and ex-journalists have noted. As former *New York Times* reporter A. H. Raskin (1967) described the syndrome: "The press prides itself—as it should—on the vigor with which it excoriates the malefactors in government, unions and business, but its own inadequacies escape both its censure and its notice."

Rare is the newspaper with a reviewer who writes columns about print journalists, but rarer still may be a newspaper with an active television columnist who avoids review and commentary about *broadcast* news operations in that newspaper's own market. David Shaw of the *Los Angeles Times* is one of a tiny number of newspaper people reporting regularly to readers about print (as well as broadcast) journalism. When his newspaper first appointed him to cover the news media, he reported noticing immediately that his newsroom colleagues suddenly began watching him nervously and treating him with muted hostility (Shaw, 1977).

Tradition meets the ombudsman. Only about one in 50 American newspapers has an ombudsman (*ombudsman* is a Swedish term meaning a kind of "honest broker") in the newsroom for the reader. In 1967, the Louisville *Courier-Journal* was the first U.S. newspaper to institute a readers' ombudsman. Since the late 1970s, however, few other newspapers have hopped onto the ombudsman bandwagon. In addition, the turnover among ombudsmen has been extraordinarily high on newspapers such as the *Washington Post*. However, sometimes this is by design; it is regarded as a way to encourage independence by ombudsmen who know they have limited terms.

Apparently, being an ombudsman can put one into conflict with various factions of staffers and editors. Despite the fact that the typical ombudsman has an extraordinary 30 years of newspaper editing and reporting experience, "the staff appears to insist that the ombudsman earn his spurs by suffering through an initial period of skepticism in the newsroom" (Mogavero, 1982). Journalists' defensiveness markedly increases when the ombudsman actually tells the newspaper's reader about what has been found:

> Newspaper people are very, very sensitive to internal criticism and they are particularly sensitive to criticism in print [Charles Seib, *Washington Post* ombudsman, quoted in Mogavero, 1982].

> I was managing editor . . . and I had great problems with the way [the ombudsman] dealt with our people in some of those [published] columns. I thought he was too specific about laying blame there. One of our employees would read that [published] column and he wouldn't be good for a day. His whole day would be shot. We could not get any production out of him at all [Don Brandt, *Wilmington News-Journal*, who eliminated the published critiques when he became ombudsman himself; quoted in Mogavero, 1982].

Tradition meets the press council. The press council is another journalistic innovation whose popularity seems to have waned. In the United States, press councils have taken two general forms: (1) an audience-oriented local press council and (2) a quasi-judicial state or national news council.

Local press councils seem partly to have served as audience feedback groups for newspaper publishers and editors, since each local council comprised members of the newspaper's community. Although publishers often appointed these persons, universities and private funding agencies generally initiated the press councils themselves. Publishers were recruited to set up the local press council on an "experimental" basis. When the experiment was over, generally the press council was, too.

Unlike local press councils, news councils serve an almost judicial role, receiving and investigating complaints from citizens, from figures in the news, and from others who may have been affected by the news media. The Minnesota Press Council is the only state news council in existence today. Newspapers in Oregon and a few other states have flirted with the notion of a state news council, but ultimately rejected the idea. The Minnesota Press Council, unlike the more famous and controversial National News Council, has had fairly uniform support from the news media in its "jurisdiction," though it took a while for Minnesota broadcasters to join newspapers in funding the council.

In contrast to the broad support found in Minnesota, the National News Council (NNC) started with many strikes against it and never really overcame its difficulties during its approximately 10-year existence. From the start, such media heavyweights as *Time* magazine, both national wire services, ABC News, and the *New York Times* opposed the NNC. Not only did these organizations refuse to provide information when the NNC requested it, they also urged the rest of the news industry to refuse to allow any of their senior journalists to serve on the NNC. As was the case with the local press council idea, the National News Council was initiated and pushed by academicians[3] and foundation support. Though many news organizations eventually decided to cooperate with the NNC, and several even allowed senior staff to serve on it as journalistic members, the NNC was not in any sense the darling of the media.

Lack of support for either the local press council or the news council seems often to run through newsrooms and into the offices of top management. As news researcher John Polich (1974) found in a national survey, most newspaper publishers said they probably would print the findings of news councils—largely in the spirit of fair play—but they saw little or no need for such councils: "These are striking reservations to be harbored by the men whose decisions will nurture through cooperation and publicity whatever power news councils gain."

Since the NNC had no legal authority, its principal means of pressing for change in journalism was through the power of publicity. Presumably, when findings critical of media performance were published, journalists and management would be embarrassed enough to make changes. However, NNC findings weren't often publicized by the general news media, especially when the case being investigated wasn't thought by editors to be interesting to the general audience. Thus the power of publicity was weakened almost from the start by news media disinterest. For only a part of its history, the NNC's findings were published, but only in one of two journalism publications, each with limited circulation among professionals and neither readily available to the general public.

Journalism reviews. We've seen so far that the ombudsman movement has been slow to spread and that the news council/press council movement has, if anything, lost ground. To this list of symptoms of journalistic resistance, we should probably add the sharp decline of the once-flourishing local journalism review as another potential source of criticism and new ideas about the practice of journalism. Local journalism reviews sprang up in the mid-to-late 1960s, vigorously challenging the journalistic status quo. Often, these were written by—and for—working journalists in media-rich places such as Chicago.

With the disappearance of most of the local reviews, the review field has been mostly left to national publications such as the *Columbia Journalism Review, Nieman Reports,* and the *Washington Journalism Review.* A national review, with limited space and a need to find nationally relevant cases—the outcomes of which can be wrapped up in a single issue—obviously cannot replace local reviews, with their ability to follow up and to pursue, poke, and prod specific newspapers and broadcasters.

Making ends of techniques. Another reason tradition weighs heavily is that, over generations of journalists, journalistic "means" have become "ends" in themselves as their original purposes are forgotten. The longer a traditional practice remains in place, the more likely it is that it will become an end in itself. This transformation was clearly revealed when Mills (1983) asked a sample of newspaper journalists to describe in their own words the types of situations in which they would face "ethical" decisions: "For the vast majority of respondents in the survey, ethics were viewed as a question of adherence to a rather narrowly defined code of professional behavior. For most, it is not an exaggeration to say that ethics equated with 'objective' news coverage."

In newspaper parlance, "objective" news coverage means that a news story must have certain characteristics. For example, all "opinion" statements must be attributed to a source—they cannot come from the reporter. Further, opinion statements favoring one side should be balanced by efforts to obtain statements from the "other" side. In any event, however, it is a "fact" that Source A said whatever was said. The reporter is held accountable for the accuracy of this quote, not for the quote itself. In other words, a checklist of procedures and practices is substituted for—and becomes the equivalent of—the end itself: being "ethical." In the Mills study, quoting sources accurately was one way to be "ethical."

Sociologist Michael Schudson (1978) and many others suggest that the reasons underlying certain very long-lived journalistic practices—such as the doctrine of objectivity and how it is achieved—have been forgotten as succeeding generations of journalists have been taught to "follow the rule book." If specific rules of "objectivity" have become ends in themselves for many journalists, one can imagine how journalists might first react to the suggestion that such rules should be reexamined.

When change occurs. None of this means that there have been no changes in journalistic practices. Changes have tended, however, to have one thing in common: they were induced by "outside" forces acting upon journalists, such as new newsroom technology, competition from new media, and new ownership structures.

In the 1960s, television news became such a force when it began to eat into newspaper audiences—continuing a trend already begun earlier by radio news—by giving some subscribers the impression that one no longer really needed newspapers for the news. Only belatedly, and only after much of the damage had already been done, have we seen the newspaper industry deemphasize "breaking" national-international news and increase its emphasis of local and/or more complete reports.

A second example of change induced by "outside" factors is the growth of reporter autonomy in moderate to small television news operations. The introduction of electronic news gathering (ENG) technology had the effect of allowing ambitious TV reporters to become the editors of their own news tapes.

A third example: The introduction of video display terminals (VDTs) and electronic keyboards at newspapers didn't always go smoothly. Once introduced by newspaper managements, however, VDTs and computer storage of a reporter's half-completed stories and confidential notes led to a whole set of new norms to protect the privacy of this electronic material. It is, for example, usually considered deeply discourteous for anyone to stand behind a writer and view what is going up on the screen. It is also considered deeply discourteous for editors to call up on their own screens what reporters are writing—except at the invitation of the writer.

Fourth, in recent years, marketing researchers and the news media have discovered each other. Based on their audience research, "news doctors" advise local television newspeople about everything from the clothes and makeup they wear to the kinds of stories they report. News doctoring, as one might expect, is not very popular among most TV journalists, but the journalists generally aren't the ones who ask for outside consultants—management does that. In newspapers, similar management-ordered marketing research has guided many newspapers to create new special-interest "news" sections and advertising inserts in an effort to hang on to readers and beat back the competition from free, advertising-filled shoppers, direct-mail advertising, and so on.

Each of these changes was brought about by outside forces, combined with, in some cases, high-level management decisions. If the marketplace is such an outside force, can't it produce the changes in journalism that might be needed? In other words, maybe we don't need to have critics if the marketplace can force news media to make the changes consumers want.

It is doubtful, however, that many consumers in a community want their locally owned newspaper to be absorbed by a chain. That process, nevertheless, impelled by economic/marketplace forces that go well beyond consumer "demand," has been going on for years. Consumer demand, in other words, is only one economic factor in the media marketplace. The absorption of ever more media into ever-larger media conglomerates is a process that responds to economic factors going well beyond consumer demand. (Once again, empirical research provides some evidence about the consequences of such changes in *reducing* both the diversity of news content and the audience's knowledge of public affairs. Very few would argue that reducing the audience's knowledge of public affairs is an improvement of any kind.)

CONCLUSIONS

Throughout media history, it has been far easier to find critical statements than critical analysis concerning the news media. Critical analysis is characterized by appeals to standards and values that can be understood and shared by everyone and uses methods that are at least revealed to everyone. Further, whatever criticism or praise results from this analysis also is freely shared with journalists, other critics, and the public. This is a formidable list of criteria to be fulfilled by critical analysis.

Self-examination through "internal" mechanisms of criticism, such as the ombudsman and the news council, has met resistance from journalists themselves. This resistance has been especially strong when journalists have felt that the results would be shared with the general public. "External" mechanisms of criticism have also met with resistance from journalists, who claim the would-be critic "doesn't know the business."

The news media need to improve and change. Their role is central in complex modern societies. Changes tend to have occurred as a result of outside forces, but there's little question that the economic and technological forces producing these changes have had little or no relationship to the quality of news media performance. Therefore, it is essential that a tradition of sustained, high-quality critical analysis be created as a counterbalance.

As we shall see in the next chapter, journalists and media management are not the only obstacles blocking the way to that tradition of critical analysis. There is little consensus among critics themselves on values, standards, and methods.

NOTES

1. Most of the quotations opening the chapter are from Brown (1974). The Jefferson quotation is from Christenson and McWilliams (1967).

2. Other sources of support could be recognition and respect from the general public or from employers (through high pay), or a sense of glamour and importance communicated through portrayals of journalists in entertainment content. Unfortunately, polls for 40 years have shown the general public's esteem to be quite low for journalism as an occupation. Further, many journalistic sources are able neither to write nor to speak competently, yet they earn far more money than do the journalists who must cover them. While it's true that popular entertainment media sometimes portray journalists as glamorous or heroic, they are just as often depicted as a noisy, rude rabble whose stupid or insensitive questions demonstrate how far ahead of them the hero is. Consider the contrasting treatments of journalists in such films as *The Natural* or *Absence of Malice* with that in *All the President's Men.*

3. The real roots of the news council idea, in the United States at least, came from a proposal by the Commission on Freedom of the Press (1947), chaired by University of Chicago President Robert Maynard Hutchins. The Hutchins Commission reports were prepared by historians, law professors, and other academicians. Commission recommendations were met with great hostility by journalists, many of whom belittled the commission's findings because none of its members were journalists. For an interesting summary of journalists' hostility to the Hutchins Commission findings, see Blanchard (1977). It would be a serious mistake for modern-day students to believe that the "social responsibility theory" of the press—traceable directly to the Hutchins Commission—simply materialized when everybody realized it was a better idea.

REFERENCES

BLANCHARD, M. A. (1977) "The Hutchins commission, the press and the responsibility concept." Journalism Monographs 49 (May).

BROWN, L. (1974) The Reluctant Reformation. New York: David McKay.

CHRISTENSON, R. M. and R. O. McWILLIAMS (1967) Voice of the People (2nd ed.). New York: McGraw-Hill.

Commission on Freedom of the Press (1947) A Free and Responsible Press. Chicago: University of Chicago Press.

EDELSTEIN, A. S. (1966) Perspectives in Mass Communication. Copenhagen: Einar Harcks Forlag.

LEMERT, J. B. (1970) "Craft attitudes, the craft of journalism, and Spiro Agnew." Presented at the annual meeting of the Western Speech Association, Portland, OR, November 25.

LIEBLING, A. J. (1961) The Press. New York: Ballantine.

MILLS, R. D. (1983) "Newspaper ethics: a qualitative study." Journalism Quarterly 60 (Winter): 589-594, 602.

MOGAVERO, D. T. (1982) "The American press ombudsman." Journalism Quarterly 59 (Winter): 548-553, 580.

POLICH, J. E. (1974) "Newspaper support of press councils." Journalism Quarterly 51 (Summer): 199-206, 218.

RASKIN, A. J. (1967) "What's wrong with American newspapers?" New York Times Magazine (June 11).

SCHUDSON, M. (1978) Discovering the News: A Social History of American Newspapers. New York: Basic Books.

SHAW, D. (1977) Journalism Today. New York: Harper & Row.

SINCLAIR, U. (1919) The Brass Check: A Study of American Journalism. Pasadena, CA: Author.

2

THE "STATE OF THE ART" AMONG CRITICS

Each of four schools of criticism—Marxist, critical studies, empirical, and social responsibility—generally thinks it alone deserves to do the job.

Many of the noisiest criticisms of the news media are fundamentally misplaced. They often come from partisans of the political left or right and are focused almost entirely on whether the other side is being favored. "Is there a liberal bias in the news?" and "Are reporters antibusiness?" are probably the most common forms that this criticism takes, but one can fill in the blanks instead with phrases like "conservative bias" or "probusiness bias" and essentially the same misplacement would remain.

The debate about partisan bias in American news media began even before there was a United States, and it shows no sign of ending now. Accusations of partisan media bias occur at least as regularly as elections do. It should be no surprise, then, that it has become almost traditional for researchers to examine news bias in election coverage. And it is almost a tradition now to come up with surprisingly little evidence of a partisan slant to campaign news coverage.

Perhaps the most heated recent replay of this continuing theme in news media criticism comes in the debate over a purported "liberal bias" among elite East Coast journalists (Lichter et al., 1986). Basing many of their findings on a survey of 240 journalists and news chieftains at the three networks and three elite national newspapers in New York and Washington, D.C., Lichter et al. report that these journalists' political ideas are mostly pretty far to the left of center.

Critics of Lichter et al. have noted that they don't share enough information about their research methodology to allow other researchers to challenge their findings by trying to replicate them. Others assert that, even if we accept their evidence that elite journalists are politically liberal, it still doesn't follow that those liberal attitudes will be allowed to put a liberal "spin" on the news that finally emerges from those news organizations.

What the authors ignore in their portrait of media people is the media organization itself—its rules, codes and conventions—which, while not ensuring clinical objectivity, do introduce factors that prevent individuals from making the news columns their personal preserves [Dennis, 1986].

INSTITUTIONAL BIASES

It is precisely this preoccupation with biases caused by individuals' political ideology that has led so many critics to miss the genuine, systematic, institutional biases that partly result from the journalistic craft's need to protect itself against the very same noisy charges of political bias. Finally, we are beginning to see careful studies of biases in election campaign coverage—and other news as well—that are about structural and institutional biases rather than partisan ones. For example, researchers Peter Clarke and Susan Evans (1983) found that incumbent candidates for Congress had enormous advantages over their challengers in news coverage of the campaign. It didn't much matter whether the incumbent was a Republican or a Democrat—the bias favored whoever was the incumbent. Incumbents' names were mentioned far more often in news stories about the campaign. When there was coverage of the challenger, often it focused on the organization and people behind him or her, rather than on the policy issues he or she was trying to raise concerning the incumbent's record in office.

Following are some examples of institutional biases. Ironically, each is produced in part by the need for journalists to avoid the appearance of political bias.

Item: Political opinion doesn't often appear in the news unless the opinion can be attributed to "a source." In other words, this opinion cannot have come from the journalist. Supposedly, the journalist is merely relaying a source's viewpoint, and it is a verifiable *fact* that this opinion was voiced by this source. Journalists are held responsible for the accuracy of the quotes and paraphrases they use, but they minimize their vulnerability to charges of political bias by choosing the most obvious and defensible sources to quote in their stories. The more obviously "qualified" the source speaking is on that topic, the less vulnerable reporters and their editors feel their selection of that source will be. In practice, "qualified" sources tend to have appeared already in previous news stories. They also tend to be officials from near the top of bureaucratic organizations already on reporters' beats (e.g., fire and police agencies, public schools, city hall) or persons selected by those organizations to speak to the news media for them.

In effect, then, it is easier for public officials than for others to be regarded as qualified sources. This "official source" bias in the news—intended to minimize journalists' exposure to the dreaded charge of political bias—may itself have the effect of restricting the range of political ideas reported in the news (see Gans, 1980: 39-69). Generally, appropriate credentials to be a "legitimate" source are accompanied by a certain conventionality of political ideas. This bias in favor of "official" sources and against sources without credentials is, in a sense, a "nonpartisan" bias. Nevertheless, it certainly can prevent ideas from either end of the political spectrum from receiving much public attention.

Item: Journalists share a professional bias against repeating stories that lack anything "new." A policy proposed yesterday may have been news yesterday, but journalists won't treat the proposal as news today unless another source reacts or some other "new" development occurs. Despite—or perhaps even because of—this bias, we know that yesterday's news item probably would be brand new information *today* to most people.

While advertisers have no hesitation about repeating messages until they "reach and teach" the intended audience, journalists would be scandalized and embarrassed if identical news items were broadcast or printed two days in a row. What's the connection of this bias with the craft need to avoid charges of political bias? If it were possible to repeat identical news stories, journalists would have to decide *which* of them should be repeated—and which weren't "worth" repeating. This decision would open the craft to a new and slightly different charge of manipulation, slant, or bias.

There are, of course, many more media criticisms than can be treated in detail in this book. Some media critics simply are responding to the coverage they or their institutions get in the press. Some business leaders fall into this category. Media criticism is only a passing concern for them, but they are sometimes heard loud and clear. Some critics have a political or ideological agenda. Accuracy in Media, for example, is a conservative organization that often claims the mass media have a clear-cut liberal bias. Action for Children's Television is an organization that believes that much of television fare is not good for children. In their view, this is especially true of entertainment programs and advertising. Still other groups, ranging from environmental and civil rights groups to religious organizations, engage in media criticism and analysis. Attentive students will be on the lookout for both polemical and scholarly criticism. In our pluralistic system there is a lot of it, and it receives varying degrees of attention (or inattention) from the media.

In short, then, the most widely heralded and publicized criticisms stress partisan political bias, while some of the most systematic, subtle, consistent, and significant biases may occur precisely because journalists are preoccupied with forestalling those noisy charges of political bias.

CRITICISM FOR WHOM?

Media criticism doesn't exist in a vacuum. It is written by critics who have a particular purpose or point of view and it is directed to a particular audience. Media criticism aimed at high-level government decision makers will therefore differ from media criticism aimed at the general public or at journalists themselves. Who, then, should be the "users" or constituents of media criticism?

- *The public?* National publications, networks, wire services, and other media write about "the media," and then expose the mass audience to the flaws and foibles of the news media. This has a kind of consumer "education" function for society.
- *The journalists themselves?* If improvements are to be made in journalistic practices, it will be journalists who will carry out those changes.
- *Journalism teachers?* If new ways of doing things are to be taught in journalism education, these will be the people who will teach them.
- *Other critics?* They are, or perhaps ought to be, each critic's peer group.

Good cases can be made for critics addressing the mass audience and/or journalists. Something of a case can be made for addressing journalism teachers, although about half of journalists with college degrees enter the craft without having been journalism majors in college (Weaver and Wilhoit, 1986). But hardly anybody would argue seriously that the chief audience for criticisms of the media should be other critics. Yet, it is hard *not* to believe that's who many critics are writing for. When this happens, it is hard to be optimistic that—insightful as they may be—these critics have any chance at all of influencing news practices.

Clearly, if we are interested in producing change in news media practices, criticism should be addressed to the news media themselves and to the people who educate journalists. And if we are interested in providing both warnings and coping skills to news media audiences, then we should address our media criticisms to the mass audience as a kind of "consumer protection" service.

Only occasionally does it make much sense to address media criticisms to another audience: *decision makers in government.* I recall doing this only twice in my career, once with regard to the Pacific Time Zone audience's inability to determine when the network news had been taped and delayed three hours for replay in the West, and once with regard to the effects of network news election projections on Western voters. In the first case, all that would have been required would have been reinstatement of a former Federal Communications Commission rule that audiences be notified of tape delays on programs (like the news) in which timeliness is important. In the second case, a bill requiring simultaneous closing times for presidential elections—combined with a voluntary agreement by networks—was the solution being considered. Direct government attempts to regulate news media projections are restricted by First Amendment considerations.

DIVIDED, WE FAIL

If God had told Noah to match up each school of media criticism with one other before leading them in pairs onto the Ark, they'd probably all have drowned first. Several schools of media criticism don't seem to be on speaking terms with one another.[1] Worse, they may not even be on *listening* terms. Their ideas about what other schools are doing, saying, and thinking may have been stereotypical to begin with, and even if they weren't, each critical school hasn't been listening to some of the others for so long that it inevitably risks being out of touch with what currently is being assumed, thought, done, and said there. As a result, caricatures—instead of real people and ideas—often are being discussed and discarded. (A special summer 1983 issue of the *Journal of Communication*—quite appropriately titled "Ferment in the Field"—conveys some of the flavor of the many disputes being waged among media critics. While the articles are not all well written and some of them repeat points already made in other articles, reading them is an eye-opening experience. These people seem very angry at what they think the others believe and do.)

At the risk of creating a set of caricatures for you, let me sketch four distinctly different schools of thought about the news media. They appear to differ fundamentally concerning both their assumptions about the news media and how to do critical analyses.

(1) *Marxist*-oriented criticism looks at the news media—and mass media generally—as one of several mechanisms through which, by the creation of a nearly universal false consciousness, subordinate groups and classes are deceived into cooperating with social and economic arrangements that benefit ruling elites. To Marxists, journalists' craft attitudes reflect a specialized false consciousness that both justifies ideas such as "objectivity" and distracts newspeople from realizing that craft practices make it easier for the masses to be deceived. Strong divisions exist even within the Marxist camp, but to some extent there is overlap, interaction, and interchange between Marxist and the cultural/critical studies (CCS) school.

(2) *Cultural/critical studies,* in its British, Continental, and American manifestations, has been heavily influenced by Marxist analyses. CCS tends to endorse the idea of a false consciousness and the role of the media in creating and maintaining it. If anything, CCS critics stress the centrality of the media role more than Marxists do. They tend to assume that media messages have great—though often subtle and indirect—power. Therefore, CCS is especially emphatic about analyzing (a) media content, (b) who decides what content is produced, and (c) what rationales are given for those decisions. In effect, although the audience's ability to reinterpret media content gets rhetorical support, CCS tends to assume that close examination and interpretation of overt and covert messages in media will also tell us what the meanings are that audiences attach to those messages.

In emphasizing the indispensability of the media somewhat more than do the Marxists, CCS also tends not to focus on other institutions and arrangements that supplement or complement the media's consciousness-maintenance role. On the one hand, compared to the Marxists, CCS also tends currently not to be as quick to connect media content to the specific political-economic structures maintained or supported by that content. On the other hand, CCS (especially in America) tends to define its subject matter as going beyond, and being broader than, just the political and economic components emphasized by the Marxist approach.

(3) *Empirical* criticism uses "scientific" methodology to produce data-based findings that can be used to assess media performance. Empirical critics share with other empirical social scientists an admiration of the methods and achievements of the older physical and biological sciences. Generally, they also share with other empirical social scientists a belief that systematic and impartial testing of research hypotheses is virtually as feasible in the social sciences as in the older

sciences. This shared belief does not imply that all problems of human existence can be studied empirically, but it does imply that those that *can* be studied probably are *best* studied empirically.

(4) *Social responsibility*-oriented critics feel that higher standards than profitability should be applied to the news media. In fact, they argue, it is the marketplace (and larger economic forces of consolidation) that has produced an enormous problem for Western democracies. The problem: While news audience members once might have been able themselves to sort out good ideas from bad, there aren't enough different media voices now to assure that the public will receive a genuine range of ideas to sort through. Very few cities any longer have competing newspapers. Even when a city does, often both newspapers are controlled by chains whose similar principles of operation serve to reduce the potential for diversity. Network and local television news, social responsibility critics assert, is so constrained by outmoded time and format limitations that it offers little more diversity than do the two remaining national news wire services—Associated Press and a greatly weakened United Press International. Furthermore, huge media conglomerates now own TV stations and networks, satellite broadcasting, cable and pay TV systems, newspapers and radio stations, and rights to possible future media technology not as yet widely known.

As a result of these and related trends, social responsibility theory asserts that the news media must be pressed to take responsibility for bringing fair, accurate, and complete accounts to consumers who, through no fault of their own, no longer are well equipped to detect the unfair, the inaccurate, and the incomplete. If a news medium refuses to take this responsibility, it must be pressured, embarrassed, and confronted until it does. Press councils, news councils, professional education of journalists, journalism reviews, and professional ethics codes are among the available mechanisms for pressure and exposure. If pressure doesn't work, at some unspecified point the threat of government action is raised by some social responsibility theorists.

Crystallized and made concrete by the famed (University of Chicago President Robert) "Hutchins Commission" report, *A Free and Responsible Press*, social responsibility theory was greeted with hostility and opposition from the media and many journalism educators (Commission on Freedom of the Press, 1947). Four decades later, however, many of the values of social responsibility theory—for example, the goal of separating news judgments from profitability concerns—are taken for granted as desirable goals in newsrooms and classrooms across the country. As a consequence, an important, consensually supported set of ethical guidelines automatically can be brought to bear on any of several identifiable kinds of news media "violations" of responsibility. The fact that, as in all human activity, actual practice in journalism sometimes differs from the ideal does little to lessen acute embarrassment when such journalistic failures come to public notice. One of the reasons this embarrassment is so acute is that news media managers and employees almost invariably proclaim that they mean to serve the public interest, not their own.

Social responsibility criticism, like the journalistic behavior it sometimes examines, habitually deals with specific anecdotal events or incidents. Journalists covering news stories tend to operate with the same kind of anecdotal data—individual stories. So social responsibility-based critics are talking in the same language and have a worldview similar to that of modern journalists themselves. Obviously, this sharing of values and ways of thinking gives social responsibility critics power to engage in "moral suasion."

It wouldn't be hard to subdivide each of these four schools of criticism into even more subtypes, but little would be added by doing so. With this warning—that we may be dealing with caricatures here— let's pretend that we can know for certain what a typical member of each school of criticism would say about each of the other three. These imaginary monologues—remember, a *dialogue* assumes that the parties are actually listening to each other—begin with Marxists talking about the other three schools of criticism.

What Marxists Might Say About Other Schools

The *cultural/critical studies* approach is somewhat useful. Unfortunately, though, some cultural/critical studies critics rely too much on receiver-oriented criteria to determine what "should" be done by the news media. Since the media already have created a false consciousness in the audience, it is meaningless for this or any other critical school to use audience reaction or audience "opinion" as any kind of guide to what the news media should do. Because the audience has already been manipulated, one cannot use the audience's false consciousness to discover what the media should do differently. And, while this may sound contradictory, CCS people tend to focus too much on the media, to the exclusion of the other structures in the society.

Empirical mass communication research panders to the existing economic-political order by trying to help media become more efficient in achieving their ends. Far from questioning the history, the ownership, and the economic interconnections between media and the system they serve, empirical researchers take all of that for granted. Truly, then, they can't see the forest for the trees!

Occasionally, empirical studies of media content may be of some limited value, but empirical audience and effects studies either support existing media by increasing their efficiency or are so narrowly focused and tunnel-visioned that they are essentially irrelevant to any genuinely critical effort.

Social responsibility critics are so preoccupied with warning about such things as concentration of media ownership that they can't see that very same concentration as a perfectly logical—and historically inevitable—development in late capitalist societies. Instead of examining the underlying historical causes of such changes, they are trying to minimize harms that are merely symptoms of the cause. In such accommodation, capitalism has a friend in the so-called social responsibility critic. Typical of their futility is that such critics try to create a special professional ethic that will somehow immunize journalists against what really are inexorable historical trends.

Further, when social responsibility critics deal with discrepancies between journalists' ethical codes and journalists' actual behavior, they are mistakenly assuming that journalists have any real choice. With trivial exceptions, when journalists don't behave as their ethical codes dictate, it is less a matter of ethics than of historical necessity.

What Cultural/Critical Studies Advocates Might Say About Other Schools

In reducing most of their criticisms to economic causes, *Marxists* pay too little attention to other historical and cultural causes of news media behavior. Further, the Marxists badly need to spend more time in analysis and criticism of *specific* journalistic conventions, practices, and language forms.

Empiricists have swallowed the naive notions that research "facts" can be divorced from opinion, and that the empirical social sciences can borrow—more or less intact—the methodology of the physical sciences. Knowledge—even "scientific" knowledge—is socially constructed and, therefore, not self-correcting and perfectible through hypothesis testing. Further, media empiricists worship at the altar of quantification, when far more penetrating analytical techniques are available through qualitative techniques such as those used by insightful cultural anthropologists. Finally, an empirical finding of "bad" effects covertly substitutes audience reactions for any reasoned consideration of quality or intrinsic merit in the media content itself.

To the extent that the *social responsibility* school talks in terms of ethical codes or in terms of press councils as a way of ensuring press responsibility, it ignores the melancholy fact that it may not be in the news media's own self-interest either to live up to abstract ethical codes or to support a press council. Further, both journalists and social responsibility-inspired critics share many cultural assumptions—and thus are blind to them.

What Some Empiricists Might Say About Other Schools

Marxism, as an interpretation of modern economic-political systems, violates the first principle of science: As a "theory" it does not allow itself to be challenged empirically. Persons criticizing the news media from a Marxist perspective therefore are immune to contrary evidence. This immunity produces a uniformly paranoid perspective that treats departures from the portrait it draws as trivial anomalies, rather than as challenges to the underlying Marxist perspective. Plausibility and footnotes replace hypothesis testing as the criteria for "evidence." Because of its preoccupation with the "big picture," Marxist-oriented criticism has little to say to practicing journalists that could be of any practical value in improving their craft.

It's true that the *critical/cultural studies* approach has contributed some insightful analyses of craft practices (e.g., see Tuchman, 1978). But this approach fails to prescribe a clear methodology for how such analyses are to be done and for how we are to judge the evidence produced. Often, "proof by footnote" and/or "trust my narrative about what I observed" seem to form the evidence. It is useful to know how many months the critic spent with journalists, but, by itself, that isn't good enough.

Social responsibility theory is based on untested assumptions about increased audience vulnerability because of factors such as the decline in independent media voices. Beyond these untested assumptions, many critics operating from this point of view seem to take great pride in their ignorance about empirical findings that would actually have helped them make their case.[2]

Nevertheless, social responsibility theory can be useful in providing ideas about consensual criteria that can acceptably be used to evaluate media performance—for example, diversity in the news is highly valued by social responsibility theory, as would be a refusal by the news media to allow economic self-interest to determine news decisions. The fact that a strong consensus exists among journalists in favor of criteria such as these means that, when a good case can be made that a news medium has violated these criteria, journalists can be shamed and embarrassed. Unfortunately, too many social responsibility critics try to make their cases through examples or anecdotes, forever leaving themselves vulnerable to the accusation that they selected only the examples that fit, and ignored those that didn't.

What Some Social Responsibility Critics Say About Other Schools

Marxist critics who live and work in democracies ought to thank their lucky stars that they have the freedom to examine and comment upon news media performance. Marxists seem almost completely uncaring about the importance of the First Amendment in preserving their own right to speak and write the truth as they see it. Marxist critics also don't seem to care much about anybody else's rights, either. Journalism in democracies may not be perfect, but surely Marxist critics don't propose that we adopt the kind of state—and the kind of journalism—that we see in the Soviet Union. Get serious! Marxism has failed every time it has been applied.

The *cultural/critical studies* people have nothing practical or useful to say or propose, though occasionally they say something interesting.

What a pompous lot *empiricists* are—speaking in Communication-ese, a strange and obscure tongue that nobody but the high priesthood of communicology has any reason to try to understand.

SUMMARY

Each of these four schools of thought—Marxist, critical/cultural studies, empiricist, and social responsibility—generally thinks it alone is among The Anointed. There ought to be much more cooperation among them. (One way to accomplish that is to stop thinking and talking in terms of the foregoing caricatures.) Admittedly, most of the remainder of this book is meant to stress the good points of just one of these four camps—empirically based criticism. Why? Because it has been the one most often overlooked when media criticism is considered. As a result, few critics are aware of this relevant literature—and they may therefore have missed several golden opportunities to add weight to arguments they already have been making by adding new and distinctly different kinds of evidence gathered independently by others.

NOTES

1. Besides the present author, D. Charles Whitney also has written about news media problems with an eye toward finding common ideas and themes among different schools of criticism. See Whitney (1982).

2. By no means all social responsibility-oriented critics feel this way about empirical research. Nonetheless, some of the most visible of them seem also to be the most pridefully hostile to the thought of even considering the results of empirical research. This unnecessary schism between the two schools of criticism may reflect a larger debate about whether journalism education needs to include both "theory" and "skills." Such a false distinction, it seems to me, tells us more about the people making the distinction than it does about the relative merit of their ideas.

REFERENCES

CLARKE, F. and S. H. EVANS (1983) Covering Campaigns: Journalism in Congressional Elections. Stanford, CA: Stanford University Press.

Commission on Freedom of the Press (1947) A Free and Responsible Press. Chicago: University of Chicago Press.

DENNIS, E. E. (1986) [Book review]. Columbia Journalism Review 25.

GANS, H. J. (1980) Deciding What's News: A Study of CBS Evening News, NBC Nightly News, Newsweek and Time. New York: Vintage.

LICHTER, S. R., S. ROTHMAN, and L. S. LICHTER (1986) The Media Elite. Bethesda, MD: Adler & Adler.

TUCHMAN, G. (1978) Making News: A Study in the Construction of Reality. New York: Free Press.

WEAVER, D. H. and G. C. WILHOIT (1986) The American Journalist: A Portrait of U.S. News People and Their Work. Bloomington: Indiana University Press.

WHITNEY, D. C. (1982) "Mass communicator studies: similarity, difference and level of analysis," pp. 241-254 in J. S. Ettema and D. C. Whitney (eds.) Individuals in Mass Media Organizations: Creativity and Constraint. Beverly Hills, CA: Sage.

104892

LIBRARY
COLBY-SAWYER COLLEGE
NEW LONDON, NH 03257

3

ADMINISTRATIVE AND CRITICAL MEDIA RESEARCH

Empirical research is not limited to testing whether media goals are being reached efficiently.

The looming shadow of Adolph Hitler drove many Central European intellectuals to the United States in search of political and intellectual freedom. The impact of these refugees on American intellectual history was enormous. Their numbers included psychoanalysts Bruno Bettelheim, Eric Fromm, and Karen Horney; social psychologist Kurt Lewin; economists George Katona and Peter Drucker; political theorists Hannah Arendt and Franz Neumann; writer Thomas Mann; theologian Paul Tillich—and a tiny, energetic young Marxist scholar from Vienna who thought of himself as a kind of specialist in applying mathematics to the solution of practical social problems. His name was Paul F. Lazarsfeld.

Though Lazarsfeld was largely responsible for the beginning of systematic sociological survey research in America,

> he had practically no training in sociology, having received his university degree in applied mathematics. In his native Vienna, he had been an ardent socialist youth leader and organizer; yet he proved very adept, after coming here, in harnessing the resources of American business to the task of developing social research. He is renowned as the father of sophisticated studies of mass communications and of the factors that lead people to make choices between political candidates or between competing products; yet he was not really interested in these substantive areas but [in] . . . developing appropriate methodologies for the social sciences [Coser, 1984: 110].

Before he came to the United States on a Rockefeller traveling fellowship in 1933, Lazarsfeld had learned that he could use a research center to provide a precarious existence for himself—and for his friends and companions in the Austrian socialist movement. Realizing that the University of Vienna could provide scant support for his Vienna Research Center, Lazarsfeld and his politically radical colleagues raised support money by doing market studies for businesses. In addition, keeping the research center afloat allowed Lazarsfeld and his colleagues to do a major study of the unemployed, "infused with the compassionate socialist convictions of its authors" (Coser, 1984: 112).

Lazarsfeld arrived in America during the middle of the Great Depression. Eventually, he was able to find a job as director of the University of Newark's new Research Center. Once again, as in Vienna, Lazarsfeld was expected to raise a large part of his—and everyone else's—salary and operating funds from outside sources. His first task was to analyze survey data already collected for the National Youth Administration. Soon, government agencies funded studies of unemployment in New Jersey and, eventually, some funds came in for market research studies.

It was becoming clear to Lazarsfeld that those in charge of the new and hugely successful medium of radio knew little about its astonishingly large but faceless mass audience. He moved to Princeton to codirect its new Office of Radio Research and, in 1939, the operation became the Bureau of Applied Social Research at Columbia University in New York City, the center of the rapidly growing radio industry. Lazarsfeld did much to establish large-scale audience survey research as a tool for media analysis in the United States. Much of the support for the Bureau—and, crucially, for numerous graduate students in sociology—came from foundation and industry sources. Many of the projects undertaken helped answer questions raised by the media industry: how to sample media audiences, how to measure audience size (a predecessor to our modern "ratings" systems), how to assess the advertising impact of media, whether or not—and how—the media influenced voters during political campaigns, how to pretest "pilot" broadcast programs, and how consumers decide to give new products a try. It's no wonder, then, that Wilbur Schramm (1967) called the Bureau "for 20 years . . . the liveliest center of communication research in America."

When Columbia accepted Lazarsfeld's proposal to establish what would become the Bureau there, it also gave him a "courtesy" appointment in the Department of Sociology. Sociology faculty had been looking for a "senior" faculty member, but could not agree on whether the professor should be a "pure theorist" or an "empirical" sociologist. Therefore, they decided to hire two "junior" faculty—one pure theorist (a fellow named Robert K. Merton) and one empirical type (Lazarsfeld).

All faculty hiring decisions should turn out as well. Both Lazarsfeld and Merton became towering figures in the social sciences. For the two men, who might have been typecast as antagonists ("theory versus numbers"), a period of productive cross-fertilization began, though not right away. Their association didn't really begin until late in 1941, when Merton and his wife showed up for a "get-acquainted" evening at the Lazarsfelds'. As they arrived, Merton found himself whisked downtown with Lazarsfeld to a radio station, where Lazarsfeld was testing audience reactions to a federally sponsored prewar propaganda program. Merton soon found himself conducting the postshow interviews instead of enjoying a comfortable dinner at the Lazarsfelds' apartment. Lazarsfeld then inveigled Merton to "phone the ladies and let them know we're still tied up." The pair then adjourned "to the Russian Bear and talked . . . until long after midnight" (Lazarsfeld, 1975: 36). Almost against his will, Merton found himself drawn more and more into projects at the Bureau. Eventually, he was to become for a time its codirector and de facto administrator.

Lazarsfeld described himself as a "Marxist on leave" in the United States (Coser, 1984). While in Vienna, he had already found his mathematical skills to be useful when applied to the analysis and solution of social problems. In Europe, he could address himself to two partially overlapping audiences: socialists and academics. However, when he came to the United States, there was no socialist movement comparable to that in Europe. There was, however, Franklin Delano Roosevelt's New Deal—a political program with strong intentions of correcting and ameliorating some of the social consequences of unrestrained capitalism. It should have been no surprise, then, that Lazarsfeld's American academic career at Newark began with the analysis of social problems, using funds from Roosevelt's National Youth Administration. Given that he was, for a long time, very much on the untenured fringe of some already economically hard-pressed colleges and universities during the Great Depression, it also should have been no surprise that Lazarsfeld would go after "soft" money from outside sources—just as he had been forced to do in Vienna.

Given his view of himself as a "Marxist on leave," it also should be no surprise that Lazarsfeld was less interested in the many substantive problems he and the Bureau investigated than he was in developing and refining the tools of social science. Despite the landmark studies Lazarsfeld and his colleagues contributed to the mass communication literature, at the time Lazarsfeld's intellectual ambitions had more to do with developing and legitimizing social scientific techniques than they did with the commercial or academic topics being analyzed with those techniques. At one of the Bureau's annual Christmas parties, the graduate students' skit condensed Lazarsfeld's views roughly as follows (slightly modified from Coser, 1984: 118):

Lazarsfeld (as played by student): "I've got great news! My wife just had a baby!"

"Is it a boy or a girl?" he was asked.

"I don't know—all I care about is the *method*!"

The Bureau directly and indirectly influenced the commercial media tools we are used to seeing today: broadcast rating systems, readership studies, controlled previews of broadcast "pilots" or "test" ads to determine audience reactions, and so on. Lazarsfeld and the Bureau also introduced many now-common research techniques to the academic world as well.

In any event, Lazarsfeld eventually was scathingly criticized by Marxist and cultural/critical studies writers for doing "administrative" research that might further the goals of the media industries. Ironically, it was Lazarsfeld who, in 1941, seemed to have coined the term "administrative" research and who conceded that administrative research didn't challenge the goals of the media. Lazarsfeld also wrote in a 1948 *Journalism Quarterly* article that "we academic people always have a certain sense of tight-rope walking: at what point will the commercial partners find some necessary conclusion too hard to take and at what point will they shut us off from the indispensable sources of funds and data?" (Lazarsfeld, 1972b: 124).

Notice that, by 1948, Lazarsfeld seemed to be implying that at some point even administrative research findings would *compel* the researcher to draw "necessary" conclusions that could threaten the interests of the media industry. This additional possibility for industry-sponsored administrative research either had not occurred to Lazarsfeld at the time of his 1941 article or we shall have to add it to a list of ambiguities he created in that first article.

In the field of media criticism, probably no distinction has been as heavily used—and as often abused—as the 1941 distinction made by Lazarsfeld between what he termed "administrative" and "critical" media research. While Lazarsfeld suggested in many ways in his argument that both terms could refer to empirical research, later writers have virtually preempted the term "critical research" and divorced it from any reference whatever to empirically based research. Selective recall of what Lazarsfeld wrote has been so complete that today one uses the term "critical research" at one's peril to refer to *empirical* media research. Meanwhile, the terms "administrative" and "empirical" seem to have become locked together like Siamese twins.

ADMINISTRATIVE RESEARCH

When it is empirical, administrative research about the mass media is done to determine ways of achieving the goals of media management. Of course, not all administrative research was commissioned by media organizations. A good deal was initiated by the government to assess the impact, effect, and use of media in such enterprises as information campaigns. The goals themselves are not at issue. Sometimes, alternative methods of achieving a goal are compared. However, often what is going on is that some sort of test is made of whether the existing method does the job, not a comparison of several methods.

A classic example of administrative media research is a field experiment conducted for a daily newspaper in Oregon by Galen R. Rarick (1967). In a series of "split-run" tests conducted over a number of days, Rarick tested whether or not such things as the size of the headline changed the amount of readership a news story received: Half the subscribers received the story with a small headline; the others received it with the larger one. In other tests on other days, the paper manipulated the location of the story on a given page, the story's distance from the front page, and a variety of other newspaper makeup cues that supposedly raise or lower readership of an article. Each of these makeup cues was tested in multiple split-run studies. Obviously, Rarick was not questioning the goal of the newspaper to gain readership for its "top" stories. Instead, this series of split-run experiments tested whether each makeup cue actually made a difference in readership of that story. In other words, *effectiveness or efficiency was the criterion.*

Lazarsfeld didn't make clear that a special kind of criticism *can* come from administrative research. When what the media do is *not* efficient or effective—as *effective* is defined by the research—the resulting criticism can be scathing, and painfully so. The Nielsen television ratings can be thought of as administrative research, but that definitely does not prevent producers and network vice presidents from squirming uneasily when ratings plummet.

In other fields (such as crime prevention or public health, for example) the reader may encounter the term *evaluation research.* Once again, in such research what is being evaluated is the efficiency or effectiveness of a given program in achieving whatever goal has been established for it. And once again, controversy and criticism seem constrained to whether or not a given program works.

Administrative research isn't always financed by the media organization, as we pointed out earlier. Sometimes, it isn't done explicitly for any particular media agency. For example, after World War II, psychologist Carl Hovland's research at Yale on variables that might produce attitude change examined some then-current theoretical issues about persuasion. In the sense that it examined theoretical issues, it was "basic," not applied, research. Nevertheless, had Hovland's group found some of the "magic keys" to persuasion, we can be sure that communicators would have made use of those keys. Clearly, the Yale "basic" research program was administrative in character because it tried to find ways to achieve a goal (persuasion) in which media had a vested interest.

CRITICAL RESEARCH

To repeat a point made earlier, Paul Lazarsfeld helped create and build one of the first major empirical social scientific research centers in the United States by doing what he, himself, would call administrative research. Lazarsfeld seemed to be using his distinction between administrative and critical research to appeal to some of his former academic colleagues who had also escaped Hitler's reach. In effect, he seemed to be saying, "I know that I've been doing administrative research, but I have some ideas about critical research. . . . Won't you at least listen?"

Between the lines throughout a series of essays about "critical sociology" (reprinted in 1972), one can sense Lazarsfeld's hurt reactions to some former colleagues' rejection of his research career. In his 1941 article, Lazarsfeld conceded that not much critical (empirical) research was being done at that time. Nevertheless, he clearly believed that it could and should be done. Unfortunately, his recipe for what sort of empirical media studies would be "critical" was not as clear and straightforward as it is possible to be today.

Nonetheless, Lazarsfeld (1972a: 165) did anticipate an important modern trend in empirically based criticism of the news media:

If we study the effects of communication, however fine methods we use, we will be able to study only the effects of radio programs or printed material that is actually being distributed. Critical research will be especially interested in such material as never gets access to the channels of mass communication: What ideas and what forms are killed before they ever reach the general public . . . ?

Many of the studies we'll be looking at in this book are precisely about what is *not* in the news. What does *not* appear in the news media can be more important than what does. Audiences can't react to things they don't hear about.

How does one study things that don't happen? Fortunately, journalism as an occupation seems ideally suited to documenting silences and avoidances. We are getting to be quite clever at doing this. In general terms, what we do is to establish some baseline against which the absence of a certain kind of media content shows up in stark relief. To illustrate—if the census tells us that blue-collar workers are heavily present in the community, we can ask whether blue-collar workers appear in the same proportions *in the news.* Methods of establishing baselines vary a great deal, depending on the design and purpose of the study, but the idea of a baseline against which media content is contrasted occurs again and again in empirically based critical research. As we'll see in the next chapter, one of the convenient by-products of empirical researchers' "lust" for manipulating and measuring variables is that, in creating and measuring these variables, they often are creating baselines, as well.

Once the content does appear in the media, Lazarsfeld (1972a: 166) suggests, critical researchers can "look at the content in an original way," not taking for granted the goals of the people who produced the content. Lazarsfeld implies the use of at least two standard social scientific methodologies in this discussion—content analyses and audience surveys—but concedes that his ideas about empirically based critical research are sketchy and partial.

Of course, we've had the benefit of decades more of hindsight than the pioneering Lazarsfeld had when he wrote his articles in the late 1930s and early 1940s.

WHAT EMPIRICAL CRITICISM CAN DO

Given the benefit of that hindsight, let me propose at least five distinct benefits that empirical research offers to the field of news media criticism.

(1) *Empirical research allows us to compare rhetoric with empirical "reality."* For example, when newspaper chains buy formerly independent newspapers, they often take great pains to point out that the new member of the chain retains its editorial independence. Editorial page staffers (sometimes the same people who worked there before the acquisition) may vehemently offer the same assertion: "The home office

doesn't interfere with our editorial page." A careful content analysis by Oregon graduate Ralph Thrift, Jr. (1977) found that after newspapers were acquired by chains, their editorials far less often vigorously argued about local issues of concern to their readership. (This study will be covered in more detail in Chapter 6.)

Journalists also speak in glowing, altruistic terms about the "adversarial" duty of journalism to question the comfortable and powerful. Yet, study after study shows that it is precisely the powerful who have access to the news, while the powerless—who may have equally appropriate and valid things to say—can gain access largely at the extreme price of having their original ideas distorted (e.g., Roshco, 1975; also see Chapter 6).

(2) *Empirical research allows us to document unexpected or unanticipated effects.* That is, we can look for effects upon audiences that may be previously unexamined or latent by-products of the "normal" ways that the news media do their jobs. For example, it appears that the more newspaper coverage there is of public affairs topics, the greater the gaps among members of the public in how much they actually know about those topics. The first linkage between news coverage and survey evidence of the knowledge gap was reported by Tichenor et al. (1970).

(3) *Empirical research allows us to bolster or support critics from other schools.* Empirical evidence can provide independently arrived at support for social responsibility-oriented critics, as well as for other schools of criticism. For example, social responsibility critics believe that the trend toward consolidated ownership of news media within a given community takes away from the audience much of its ability to compare notes, to pit one news message against another version in a rival local medium. A content analysis and audience survey by journalism professor Guido Stempel (1973) supports that assumption.

(4) *Empirical research gives other critics new and different arguments to use.* Gradually, some other critics have begun to realize that empirical results can provide baselines and benchmarks that help them make their arguments. For example, two studies in the early 1970s reported similar amounts of duplicated content (roughly 70%) in the networks' early evening weekday newscasts. What if studies done now were to show the rate of duplication to be even higher? Or lower, for that matter? The first two studies thus provide a baseline against which a later study's results can be compared. Similarly, media sociologist George Gerbner's well-known "Violence Index"—produced using content analysis—provides a standardized baseline for tracing change (if any) in the amount and type of violence on American network

television. Those who claim that televised violence is getting either "worse" or "better"—everybody from network officials to Action for Children's Television—must confront the evidence. Claimants may try to argue around that evidence, use it triumphantly, or deny its validity—but they must confront it.

Empirical evidence can reach some journalists who would otherwise like to dismiss their critics as zealots. It is hard for journalists to reject empirical evidence—at least, on grounds that it is *empirical*. After all, asking questions of people—and using other ways of "finding out"—is what journalists do, too.

(5) *Empirical research allows us to raise new questions.* No school of thought has a monopoly on what questions ought to be asked about the behavior of journalists. Already, in the mass communication literature, it is apparent that empirical findings have raised bothersome new questions about both ends and means in the news media.

REFERENCES

COSER, L. (1984) Refugee Scholars in America. New Haven, CT: Yale University Press.
LAZARSFELD, P. F. (1972a) "Administrative and critical communication research," pp. 155-167 in P. F. Lazarsfeld, Qualitative Analysis: Historical and Critical Essays. Boston: Allyn & Bacon. (Original work published 1941)
LAZARSFELD, P. F. (1972b) "The role of criticism in the management of mass media," pp. 123-138 in P. F. Lazarsfeld, Qualitative Analysis: Historical and Critical Essays. Boston: Allyn & Bacon. (Original work published 1948)
LAZARSFELD, P. F. (1975) "Working with Merton," pp. 36-66 in L. Coser (ed.) The Idea of Social Structure: Papers in Honor of Robert K. Merton. New York: Harcourt Brace Jovanovich.
RARICK, G. R. (1967) Field Experiments in Newspaper Item Readership. Eugene: University of Oregon, School of Journalism, Division of Communication Research.
ROSHCO, B. (1975) Newsmaking. Chicago: University of Chicago Press.
SCHRAMM, W. (1967) Human Communication as a Field of Behavioral Research. Palo Alto, CA: Stanford University Institute for Communication Research.
STEMPEL, G. H., III (1973) "Effects on performance of a cross-media monopoly." Journalism Monographs 29 (June).
THRIFT, R. R., Jr. (1977) "How chain ownership affects editorial vigor of newspapers." Journalism Quarterly 54 (Summer): 327-331.
TICHENOR, P. J., G. A. DONOHUE, and C. N. OLIEN (1970) "Mass media flow and differential growth in knowledge." Public Opinion Quarterly 34 (Spring): 159-170.

4

TOOLS THE EMPIRICISTS USE

Empirical critics test hypotheses about news media performance using a variety of methodologies.

Empirical mass communication researchers aren't a bunch of clones. There's lots of room for differences among them in insight, guile, and willingness to play their hunches. As Broad and Wade (1982: 223) put it in another context, "Science is not removed from the wellsprings of art or poetry."

Nevertheless, empirical researchers share some basic ways of thinking about problems—and these shared assumptions yield at least one important advantage: These researchers think about media problems in terms of *variables*. And thinking in terms of variables almost automatically means that built into their empirical research are one or more *baselines* against which media performance can be measured.

To illustrate this "baseline" idea, let's suppose we think that the three networks' evening newscasts are more alike than they should be. Suppose, then, that we do a study of how many stories the networks carry in common each weekday evening. We find that 70% of weekday evening network news items are carried by at least two of the three networks. Immediately, we are confronted with these questions: Is 70% too much duplication? Shouldn't there be at least *some* duplication? After all, it would indeed be frightening if each network seemed to be covering entirely separate and unique worlds! So, some duplication rate above zero seems justifiable, but how far above zero should it be?

In other words, we need a baseline against which the duplication rate of 70% can be compared. Ideally, that baseline would give us a way to decide whether 70% is too high or maybe even too low. Here is where we are helped by researchers' nearly automatic wish to convert the phenomena they study into variables—that is, into things that can change or vary. If 70% is the weekday duplication rate, why not compare that against a baseline rate for weekends? By so doing, we have, in effect, made day of the week into a *variable* that can take one of two values: weekend or weekday. Presumably, the networks are covering the same common world on Saturdays and Sundays as they do on Mondays through Fridays. If the duplication rate on weekends is the same as on weekdays, perhaps the duplication rate really reflects the unwavering constancy of the demands that "reality" places on journalists to cover the same world. But if the duplication rate is lower on Saturdays and Sundays than on weekdays, it would imply that at least some of the weekday duplication is *not* compelled by "reality."

In a study done at the University of Oregon, we found that the weekday duplication rate (70%) was considerably higher than that on weekends (39%) (Lemert, 1974). That lower duplication rate for weekends gives us a baseline indicator of how much duplication is compelled by the need to cover a common political-economic "reality." A weekday duplication rate higher than the weekend rate, we thus can argue, is *optional* by that amount and reflects factors such as convenience and, perhaps, a "herd instinct" among competing network journalists. Thus does the researcher's lust for variables almost automatically create baselines.

VARIABLES AND HYPOTHESES

Let us consider further this notion of variables. Why do researchers feel they must organize their empirical studies in terms of them? Once we understand this, we can analyze examples of media criticism based on the principal data-gathering methods that we have in our bag of tools.

A deceptively simple description of a "variable" goes something like this: *The properties or values of a variable can change.* In the network news study, we've already seen two variables used in the analysis—the rate of duplicated news stories and the day of the week. At least two other variables also were strongly implied—which network (ABC, NBC, or CBS) was doing the newscast, and what news stories were covered that day. Also treated as variables in that study were such things as (1) who the apparent source of the story was (e.g., a government official, an official from the private sphere, an individual with no organizational affiliation), (2) how many seconds long each story was, (3) whether the story was read by the anchor or involved a correspondent, and (4) what kinds of visuals accompanied the story (e.g., no visuals, a rear-screen projection, film but no sound, both sound and film). The terms within each set of parentheses in this list can be thought of as the *values* available to be taken by that variable.

In contrast to a variable, we can describe a *constant* as follows: *In a study, the value of a constant cannot change.* Suppose, for instance, that we wish to study the network news preferences of a sample of John

Birch Society members. (The Birch Society is an ultraconservative political organization, mainly active in the West, that achieved some notoriety and even inspired a popular folk song in the 1960s.) While which network newscast they preferred would be a variable, membership in the Society would be true of all respondents—in short, a constant. Since all respondents are Birchers, we cannot use Birch Society membership to explain any differences we see among them in the newscasts they preferred. In other words, *a constant cannot predict or explain a variable.*

We might very well be able to subdivide the Birchers in some way and to use the subdivision categories to create what is called an "independent" variable. The independent variable, unlike membership in the Birch Society, might predict which newscast is preferred. To illustrate, we could divide up the Birchers by the length of time they have been members. Length of membership would thus become our variable, but membership itself would remain a constant. Perhaps we might then find that the longer respondents have been members, the more often they prefer (say) ABC's news.

Suppose, however, that we wanted to convert membership itself into an independent variable—and thus to be in a position to use it to predict newscast preference. We could do that by interviewing one or more groups of non-Birchers. We could, for example, compare newscast preferences of Birchers against those of (say) the liberal Americans for Democratic Action. (For all practical purposes, there would be no overlap of membership between the two organizations, so if somebody belonged to the John Birch Society, we could be quite certain he or she wouldn't also belong to the ADA.) We might call this new variable something like "political group membership." This new variable would have at least two values now: ADA members and Birch Society members. We might find ADA members choosing CBS newscasts, and Birchers tending to prefer ABC newscasts.

The variable to be explained or predicted by the independent variable is called the "dependent" variable. When membership thus is allowed to become an independent variable, it is now "eligible" to try to explain the (dependent) variable: newscast preference. If ADA members were to choose CBS while Birchers chose ABC, we could say that political group membership *covaried* with newscast preference. That is, a change in the value of one variable (for instance, from ADA to Birch members) would coincide with a change in the value of the second (dependent variable)—from CBS to ABC news preference. When one value changed, the other usually would, too. They would be said to have covaried. Finding two or more variables that covary makes it possible to explore several kinds of relationships among them.

Some relationships between independent and dependent variables may be *causal*: Changes in the independent variable cause changes in the other. On the other hand, two variables may covary because they are *both caused by some other variable(s)* we may not even know about yet. And some variables may just *seem* to covary—for example, as a result of accidents of sampling.

Another dimension in which we may be able to discuss relationships between variables is *direction*. The direction of a relationship can be positive or negative. If positive, the higher (or more positive) the value taken by one variable, the higher or more positive the value taken by the other. If the relationship is negative, the higher (or more positive) the value taken by one, the *lower* (or more negative) the value taken by the other. Negative relationships can be at least as strong—and as useful for prediction—as positive relationships. Examples of a positive relationship and of a negative relationship are given below (both are imaginary).

Positive relationship between variables: The greater the number of minutes per week given by local TV news to state and local news, the more knowledge of state and local affairs the viewers will have.

Negative relationship between variables: The larger the total number of stories carried per week by their newspaper, the less likely subscribers are to have read any single story.

Hypotheses

The two examples immediately above are worded in the way that most empirical researchers would state a *research hypothesis*, a prediction that two or more variables will covary. Often, as in these examples, hypotheses will specify the direction (positive or negative) of the relationship. All research hypotheses share some basic characteristics; these are discussed below.

(1) *Research hypotheses specify or imply at least two variables.* In the two examples above, the variables are, respectively, number of minutes of state/local news per week and amount of knowledge, and total number of news stories per week and the likelihood that a given story is read. Why must research hypotheses have at least two variables? Because, as noted earlier, we can't use something that doesn't change (a constant) to explain something that does (a variable). Nor can we reverse it and use a variable to explain a constant. Remaining constant

sometimes can pose a great challenge for lovers, but it would be no challenge at all to "predict" something the value of which always remains the same.

(2) *Research hypotheses always focus on how variables relate to each other.* Descriptions of relationships tend to have embedded in them conclusions about direction, about which variable is dependent and which independent, and so on. Some hypothetical descriptions of relationships can be quite complex, especially when they involve more than two variables. For example, a relationship between the first two variables can depend on the value taken by a third. Here's an imaginary example: When citizens have faith in their political system, the more years of education they have, the *higher* their voting turnout rate will be. But when people don't have faith in their political system, the more years of education they have, the *lower* their turnout rate will be. In other words, the hypothesis states that the direction of the education-turnout relationship depends on that third variable: faith (or lack of it) in the political system.

(3) *Research hypotheses take the form of predictions, whereas most other ways of "knowing" things take the form of explanations for outcomes after they've already occurred.* Once an outcome is known, there is little or no risk. Impromptu, ad hoc explanations and "common sense" always can be made to fit what has already happened. For instance, if John starts dating Sue after Jane leaves town for two weeks, we tend to use this commonsense explanation: Out of sight, out of mind. But if John doesn't start dating anybody else and, instead, languishes in misery every day that Jane is gone, we use *this* commonsense explanation: Absence makes the heart grow fonder.

(4) *Research hypotheses have clear implications for how they can be tested, empirically, as well as for what results have to occur if each hypothesis is correct.*

DESIGNING EMPIRICAL STUDIES

We've seen why empirical critics, like social scientists in general, seem so preoccupied with variables and research hypotheses. Now it's time for a quick look at methods in the tool bag of empirical criticism, including content analysis, survey research, and experiments. (For further details about research methodology, see Kerlinger, 1973; Stempel and Westley, 1981.)

Content Analysis

This method is just what the name implies—some kind of systematic coding or categorizing of mass media content. Generally, content analysis of existing media output has the important advantage of being *unobtrusive*. The researcher generally does the analysis *after* the content has already appeared in the media. Therefore, editing and writing decisions are "natural" and unaffected by the knowledge that researchers are looking. This differs from a situation in which a researcher is stationed in the newsroom, observing the decision-making process.

Content analysis of media actually is part of a larger group of unobtrusive observations. Like media content, such things as bumper stickers, crime statistics, city water records, and legislative committee reports can be studied unobtrusively. Sometimes, media content analysis can be connected to an analysis of other records, such as crime rate records. For instance, Phillips (1980) proposes that news of suicides-cum-murders produces a "contagion" of similar crimes and that the rate of later suicide-murders is related to the amount of publicity the first one received.

Payne and Payne (1970) report that when Detroit newspapers ceased publication because of two strikes, the rate of robberies went *down*. In other words, there were more of these crimes when the newspapers were being published than when they weren't. (These authors offer almost no explanation of what it was about published newspapers that seemed to enhance crime.)

The same news content can be "coded" (that is, categorized) in many different ways—by length, subject matter, readability, internal structure, listenability, favorability to some cause, use of quotes versus paraphrasing, "vigor," balance, location on a page or in a newscast, use of value-laden terms, and so on. Generally, the hypotheses researchers have in mind will point them toward coding content along some lines and not others.

Content analysis was the method used in the previously described study of network news duplication. Content analysis also has figured prominently in several studies of what I have termed "mobilizing information" (MI) (see Lemert, 1981: chap. 6). MI is defined as any kind of information that enables audience members to act. Examples of MI include addresses or telephone numbers, meeting times and locations, recipes, gardening tips, the modus operandi for a crime, tactics used in a petitioning campaign, and brand names of easily accessible consumer products.

In a content analysis of major American newspapers, Lemert et al. (1977) found that MI typically was missing from the news when stories concerned political controversies, but often was provided when stories covered other topics. (Notice that the rate of MI in *noncontroversial* news provides us, once again, with a baseline against which we can evaluate the much lower MI rate for controversial stories.) These prominent newspapers included MI that might help the audience participate in such activities as gardening, model-building, buying common stocks, or contributing to charitable drives, but not with regard to participation in politics. Lobbyists, interest groups, and political "insiders" don't need to depend on external, public sources of MI such as the mass media—they already know how to reach key decision makers. It is primarily the public at large that depends on the media for MI. Therefore, without political MI in the media, political participation will tend to be limited to those who already have MI or can get it. As a result, when journalists withhold political MI, insiders can more easily organize, manage, and control those citizen policy demands that do reach decision makers.

Surveys

The sample survey is our second major research tool. In the survey, a representative sample of some larger population is asked a number of questions of interest to the researcher. Of course, the population that comes most readily to mind would be all adults living in (say) the United States. But there are many other, smaller populations from which it would be more cost-effective to draw a sample, rather than to do a census: U.S. journalists, New York City residents, San Francisco newspaper subscribers, everybody who voted in the last presidential election, and so on.

How one asks survey questions depends in part on whether the survey is being conducted in person, over the telephone, or by mail. But in any case, the questions asked fall into roughly four broad areas: (1) knowledge and information, (2) behavior (e.g., Did you vote? Did you see any newscasts yesterday?), (3) preferences/attitudes/beliefs, and (4) personal demographics (e.g., education, occupation, age). Each of these question areas can be used to construct variables.

Surveys can tell us how people react to, learn from, and use *existing* news media *content*. Surveys are not as well suited to telling us how people would react to media messages to which they aren't accustomed. In some cases, some of those messages could be so unusual that they've literally never appeared in the media. (This point will be important when we consider what experiments can do that surveys can't.)

Based in part on surveys, Levy and Robinson (1986) estimate that the way network TV newspeople traditionally do their stories helps explain why the "average viewer" does not understand the main points in two of every three network news stories. A separate survey done in the San Francisco Bay Area suggests that network news audiences can't recall virtually any information from the network news they've just watched. These are examples of administrative surveys that describe audience responses to existing, traditional news messages and lead to criticism of them for their ineffectiveness.

Surveys of journalists also are useful. Lacy and Matusik's (1983) survey of reporters employed by four Texas suburban newspapers found that only one in every ten story ideas came from the journalists themselves. The authors conclude that sources who don't fit into traditional news "beat" categories are unlikely to be sought out for story ideas. In addition, potential sources who lacked affiliation with organized groups also seemed to fall through the cracks.

Simultaneous surveys of both journalists and their audiences obviously can compare how much each group knows about the other. News sources also have occasionally been surveyed by media critics, especially in connection with checks on how accurate sources think stories were.

Experiments

Like surveys, experiments often have been used to study either audience responses or journalists' behavior. However, while audience surveys can tell us how people are reacting to current media messages, experiments potentially allow us to create messages that are *outside journalistic tradition* and to compare people's reactions to them with their reactions to the more standard, traditional messages. Similarly, while surveys can tell us much about how journalists currently do their work, experiments may allow us to create tasks or conditions outside of the routine, and then to compare how journalists would react in that new situation against their reactions in a more "normal" writing or editing situation.

The essence of an experiment is *manipulation* (planned changes) of at least one independent variable in order to see if the manipulation makes a difference in one or more dependent variables. For instance, a researcher could expose one group of subjects to a printed news story written in the traditional inverted-pyramid style and a second group of subjects to a printed news story with exactly the same information in it, but written with a "teaser" lead and in narrative feature style. The researcher might see whether the different writing styles lead to differences between the groups in such dependent variables as learning or time spent reading the story.

Well-designed experiments have numerous controls built into them that are designed to eliminate all rival explanations for results except the experimental manipulation of the independent variable(s). Elimination of these rival explanations is what gives experiments their power and clarity. What can experimenters use to create such elegant tests? Broadly speaking, two different techniques can be employed in the design of an experiment, but each technique has various subtypes:

(1) *Equalization*—making sure that a potential independent variable has no chance to influence the dependent variable—is the first technique. One method of equalization is to turn a potential influence into a constant. If it is a constant, it cannot explain any differences among the experimental groups; in effect, it is held constant for all the groups. We would call this the *method of constancy*. In our imaginary experimental comparison of two different print newswriting styles, the information in the stories was held constant, as was the fact that both experimental stories were printed.

A second method of equalization is the measuring and matching method. In our newswriting experiment, for instance, we could match the subjects assigned to each writing style on some measure of their reading abilities. If subjects in all groups are matched in reading skills, differences between the groups on the dependent variables can't be explained by differences in reading skills.

Matching people and converting variables into constants are only two of many methods by which equalization can be accomplished. In the last analysis, after every effort at equalization has been made, the experimenter still has an ace in the hole—randomization.

(2) *Randomization* merely means that subjects are assigned "at random" (by chance) to experimental treatments. No matter what other controls are used, subjects *must* be assigned by chance to whatever experimental treatments they undergo. If chance determines which member of, for instance, a matched pair of subjects gets treatment A and which gets treatment B instead, the experimenter would have to be highly unlucky to have differences between groups A and B that were due to the luck of the draw.

Over the long haul, random assignment should produce rather similar groups of subjects—even on variables we don't know about—in every experimental group. In fact, the longer the haul, the better the odds that things will even out. In other words, the larger the number of subjects assigned by chance, the greater the odds against being unlucky.

Randomization is the last refuge of the experimenter. Even after equalization has been done, it is always possible to think of some as-yet unknown and unmeasured factor that wasn't equalized. So, since we can't equalize everything, we let randomization take care of all those unknowns for us. Without random assignment of subjects to experimental treatments, we don't really have a "pure" experiment. (See discussion of "quasi-experiments," below.)

How might an experimenter let chance determine which experimental treatment a subject will receive? Flipping a coin would be one way, if the subject can be assigned to one of only two treatments. When more than two experimental treatments are to be assigned, one might throw dice or use tables of random numbers to assign subjects to varying treatments.

While the experiment is a powerful method, most experiments pose another problem. With the power and precision of experiments comes the problem of artificiality. To illustrate this, in real life, how many times do audience members read news stories with the certain knowledge that a researcher is then going to ask questions about it? Or how many times do journalists write or edit copy with the certain knowledge that researchers are going to examine the product of their writing or editing and, most likely, ask them questions about it?

Despite the potential problem of artificiality, though, if we find that experimental groups differ from each other on some dependent variable, that difference cannot be the result of the artificiality of the "lab" situation. Why? Because, presumably, subjects in all experimental groups experienced the *same* environmental artificialities. Well-designed experiments also are increasingly likely to measure dependent variables unobtrusively, in more realistic situations where there is no apparent connection to the experiment.

Let's consider a few real examples of critical experiments.

Periodically, civil libertarians, judges, and defense attorneys have strongly criticized the news media for supposedly damaging a defendant's chances for a fair trial. Allegedly, news reports about matters that might never be admissible in court as evidence—such as a defendant's confession, prior criminal record, or lie-detector results—may prejudice potential jurors against the defendant.

Several experiments have been conducted to see what information in news stories might, indeed, prejudice people against defendants. In one experiment, Tans and Chaffee (1966) found, not too surprisingly, that the more of this unfavorable information was provided in news stories, the more willing subjects were to prejudge the defendant as guilty. Kline and Jess (1966) found that an unfavorable and inadmissible news story was mentioned and at least briefly discussed in deliberations by every law school mock jury that had been given the story. Meanwhile, "control" (i.e., baseline) mock juries did not receive the news story and, of course, didn't bring it up during their deliberations.

Earlier, we saw that a survey of newspaper reporters in Texas found most of them depending on "establishment" sources. Schwantes and Lemert (1978) performed an experiment to study the same problem. As part of what supposedly was a routine in-class writing assignment, students in a Reporting I class were given the transcript of a city council meeting and asked to write a standard inverted-pyramid-style news story about it. The main order of city business in the transcript concerned whether or not a mobile home park would be allowed to expand. Two sources testified against allowing the park to expand further. What the students didn't know was that there actually were two versions of the transcript. Half of the students were given one version and half received the other.

What was said about the mobile home park was the same in both versions (in other words, the information was held constant). What changed was how the sources were identified. In the first version, one source was testifying as a representative of a neighborhood association, while the second was speaking for himself as an affected neighbor of the park. In the second version, the identifications were reversed: The first source now was the man speaking for himself and the second was the neighborhood representative.

As expected, these midyear Reporting I students wrote stories in which the neighborhood association representative appeared higher in the story, regardless of what he said, and the person speaking "only" for himself was placed lower in the story—if the student reporters used what he said at all. One implication of such results is that what is said isn't as important to journalists as who said it. But that isn't the way it's supposed to be, according to the civics textbooks.

Field Experiments

Field experiments involve the manipulation of "real-life" media content, and they generally use survey techniques to measure and compare audience responses to each version of the content. Well-conducted field experiments thus combine the precision and control of an experiment with the realism of the survey. While field experiments can combine the best of both methods, we don't see many "pure" cases of them. Why?

For one thing, if the independent variable being manipulated is going to be some sort of message in the news, newspeople (and media managers) must be willing to cooperate. For another thing, it is expensive to create two or more versions of messages, and just as expensive to interview large enough samples of people receiving the different messages. Interviewing costs often are enlarged by the need to contact and interview experimental respondents very rapidly—perhaps before another day's newspaper arrives.

Field experiments probably can't be done for some broadcast media. Unlike radio and television newscasts, the same newspaper can be printed in different versions, to be delivered simultaneously (often called a "split-run" field experiment). In a split-run, roughly half the newspapers printed and delivered carry one version of content and the other half carry a second version. Radio and television newscasts in two or more versions can't be delivered simultaneously by the same on-air station, so the split-run idea can't be used in current on-air broadcasting research. However, it is technically feasible to do something like split-run field experiments with those cable systems that can "split" one channel's signal and send the different signals to different parts of their systems.

In a number of media situations, then, it just isn't possible to do a "pure" field experiment. But sometimes we can approximate the power and precision of the experiment, while keeping almost all of the advantages of the survey. Approximating the field experiment is the goal of what has been called the "quasi-experiment."

Quasi-Experiments

Loosely translated from the Greek, *quasi* means *almost* or *virtual*. Quasi-experiments usually have a fair amount of realism going for them, but they fall short of one or more of the characteristics of an experiment. For example, because of the fact that we can't do split-runs on a station's signal, we might broadcast one version of a message on a station in one market and the other version on another station located in another market. Presumably, we would have to be very careful to *match* (equalize) stations and markets in regard to size and composition. And, presumably, the two versions of the message would differ only with respect to what the researcher wants to manipulate.

Why would this study fall short of being an experiment? Even after matching on everything possible, we would have to use a different station to carry each message and thus we couldn't randomize each subject. Having once decided which station would carry which message, we would have lost the power to assign people randomly to each message group. People who normally would watch or listen to the station would self-select into the audience for the one version we air on that station. Self-selection is incompatible with arbitrary random assignment.

A close relative of the above design is a quasi-experiment in which a message is broadcast in one market and not in a matched "control" market. Ball-Rokeach et al. (1984) arranged for the stations in one Washington State market all to carry the same experimental program. Meanwhile, a similar community in Washington didn't receive the test broadcast of *The Great American Values Test*. (Actor Ed Asner and ABC's Sandy Hill cohosted the show, which was produced specifically for the researchers.) The show encouraged viewers to confront their own basic values, using some techniques very much outside the traditions embodied in commercial TV public affairs shows. Several unobtrusive measures of whether people acted on the test message's implications suggest that seeing the show did have a substantial impact on audience behavior. For example, donations made in response to direct-mail appeals were much greater from the "test" community than from the matched "control" community.

Combinations

Increasingly, we are finding studies in which several methods are used in combination. Lemert and Larkin (1979), for instance, combined (1) a content analysis of letters submitted to the editor with (2) a survey of the letter writers themselves, as well as a comparison group of people who had never written letters to the editor. Their content analysis revealed that letters submitted with mobilizing information in them were rejected by the editor more often than were letters without MI. Further, when the editor of the letters section explained to writers why letters with MI were rejected, he invariably singled out the presence of MI as objectionable. Not surprisingly, then, several interviews with the letter writers elicited the suggestion that some letter writers had already learned that putting MI in their letters was not the way to get letters published.

These results suggest that the editor who acts as gatekeeper is the main obstacle to MI in letters to the editor. Meanwhile, the nonwriting audience seemed more interested than either the editor or the sample of writers in having MI appear in letters columns.

Another study combining content analysis with a survey was reported by Ohio University journalism professor Guido H. Stempel III (1973). A recurrent theme in social responsibility-type criticisms of the news media is that ownership of the media has become both too centralized and too consolidated, effectively insulating the news media from local audiences. Because many decisions about what local media will do no longer are made locally, social responsibility critics assert, the economic goals of the entire media conglomerate sometimes dictate that audiences of local media may not get their money's worth.

Stempel's empirical test took advantage of the fact that a single company in Zanesville, Ohio, owned the city's only newspaper, its only radio station, and its only television station. For that ever-necessary baseline, Stempel created an independent variable—number of competing ownerships—by comparing Zanesville with two other matched Ohio cities, Steubenville and Portsmouth. Steubenville had one ownership for the newspaper and a second ownership for radio and television. Portsmouth had three competing ownerships. Thus Stempel's content analysis could compare the amount of duplicated news content for each city, and the survey part of his study could compare how much knowledge people in each city had about current public affairs.

Stempel reported that news content was more diverse and comprehensive in the two multiple-ownership cities. Moreover, the survey showed that the people of Zanesville were less well informed about current public affairs than were the people of the other two Ohio cities. Stempel's (1973: 29) critical conclusion: "The people of Zanesville were not well served by the media monopoly."

In a critical study of a national sample of 82 contested races for Congress, Clarke and Evans (1983) combined content analysis of newspaper coverage with a survey of local journalists who edited and wrote news about those races. The authors conclude that journalistic inertia thwarted any possibility of a genuine challenge to incumbents. Indeed, what little coverage there was of challengers tended to ignore the policy and job performance issues that challengers were trying to raise about incumbents.

Each of the examples above combined content analysis with a survey, and it would be possible to provide many more examples of this particular combination of methods. However, it is quite possible to use other combinations. For instance, several researchers have fused experimental methodology with content analysis. In this combination, what often happens is that the kind of content produced by journalists is treated as the dependent variable and some other factor—such as the writer's prejudices, the newspaper's editorial policy, or whether or not the story concerned political controversy—is manipulated as the independent variable (see, for example, Kerrick et al., 1964; Lemert, 1984).

It is even possible to combine experiments with quasi-experiments for critical purposes. I conducted one quasi-experiment for which I resurrected subjects from past experiments for a quasi-experimental field test (Lemert, 1981). Based on both the experimental and the quasi-experimental data, I argued that Pacific Coast audiences were, in effect, being deceived into believing that they were getting the network evening news direct from the East. Taken together, both the experiments and the field test of the televised announcement showed that the best way to correct for the mistaken belief was to broadcast a very specific (and honest) "news delay" announcement. That announcement, broadcast for a month in the test community, said that the network newscast had been delayed and was being rebroadcast in the Pacific Time Zone. The Federal Communications Commission requires no such announcement as things now stand, even though it is very clear that the perceived recency and timeliness of newscasts are important to news audiences.

SUMMARY

Empirical researchers have a lust for variables. The value of a variable can change. Something with an unchanging value (a constant) cannot possibly explain or predict something with a changing value (a variable). For many reasons, the fact that something is a variable implies that it may be valuable to try to predict the value it takes. To try to do that requires that another variable (an independent variable) be tested to see if it predicts values taken by the dependent variable. A research hypothesis spells out a possible relationship between independent and dependent variables. Empirical research uses a variety of methods to test research hypotheses: content analyses, surveys, experiments, field experiments, quasi-experiments, and various combinations of these methods.

STUDY EXERCISES

Below are listed some critical statements about the news media. You'll note that each statement probably could be tested, empirically, but the statement would have to be recast for that purpose.

(1) Reword or rework the ideas in statements a through d below so that now you have *two variables* in each of them. What are they? List them and describe at least *two values* each variable can take.

(2) Now, reword the entire statement so that it is in research hypothesis form.

(3) Does your hypothesis create a baseline to be used for evaluation and criticism? Why or why not?

(4) What method or methods do you think could be used to test each research hypothesis?

    (a) Women still aren't covered very often as news sources by public affairs reporters.

    (b) Overall, recent American films display a very mixed attitude toward journalism as a field when journalists are portrayed in them.

    (c) Advertisers don't march into newsrooms any more and threaten to cancel all their ads—it's more subtle than that now.

    (d) News executives get very nervous when several reporters jointly come in to question editorial decisions about not doing or using a story.

REFERENCES

BALL-ROKEACH, S., M. ROKEACH, and J. W. GRUBE (1984) The Great American Values Test: Influencing Behavior and Belief Through Television. New York: Free Press.

BROAD, W. and N. WADE (1982) Betrayers of the Truth: Fraud and Deceit in the Halls of Science. New York: Simon & Schuster.

CLARKE, P. and S. H. EVANS (1983) Covering Campaigns: Journalism in Congressional Elections. Stanford, CA: Stanford University Press.

KERLINGER, F. N. (1973) Foundations of Behavioral Research. New York: Holt, Rinehart & Winston.

KERRICK, J. S., T. E. ANDERSON, and L. B. SWALES (1964) "Balance and the writer's attitude in news stories and editorials." Journalism Quarterly 41 (Summer): 207-215.

KLINE, F. G. and P. H. JESS (1966) "Prejudicial publicity: its effect on law school mock juries." Journalism Quarterly 43 (Spring): 113-116.

LACY, S. and D. MATUSIK (1983) "Dependence on organization and beat sources for story ideas: a case study of four newspapers." Newspaper Research Journal 5 (Winter): 9-16.

LEMERT, J. B. (1974) "Content duplication by the networks in competing evening newscasts." Journalism Quarterly 51 (Summer): 238-244.

LEMERT, J. B. (1981) Does Mass Communication Change Public Opinion After All? Chicago: Nelson-Hall.

LEMERT, J. B. (1984) "News context and the elimination of mobilizing information: an experiment." Journalism Quarterly 61 (Summer): 243-249, 259.

LEMERT, J. B. and J. P. LARKIN (1979) "Some reasons why mobilizing information fails to be in letters to the editor." Journalism Quarterly 56 (Autumn): 504-512.

LEMERT, J. B., B. N. MITZMAN, M. A. SEITHER, R. HACKETT, and R. H. COOK (1977) "Journalists and mobilizing information." Journalism Quarterly 54: 721-726.

LEVY, M. R. and J. P. ROBINSON (1986) "The 'huh' factor: untangling TV news." Columbia Journalism Review 25 (July-August): 48-50.

PAYNE, D. E. and K. P. PAYNE (1970) "Newspapers and crime in Detroit." Journalism Quarterly 47 (Summer): 233-239, 308.

PHILLIPS, D. P. (1980) "Airplane accidents, murder, and the mass media: towards a theory of imitation and suggestion." Social Forces 58 (June): 1001-1024.

SCHWANTES, D. L. and J. B. LEMERT (1978) "Media access as a function of source-group identify." Journalism Quarterly 55 (Winter): 772-775.

STEMPEL, G. H., III (1973) "Effects on performance of a cross-media monopoly." Journalism Monographs 29 (June).

STEMPEL, G. H., III and B. H. WESTLEY (1981) Research Methods in Mass Communication. Englewood Cliffs, NJ: Prentice-Hall.

TANS, M. D. and S. H. CHAFFEE (1966) "Pretrial publicity and juror prejudice." Journalism Quarterly 43 (Winter): 647-654.

5

THE COMMON BOND: EMPIRICAL AND SOCIAL RESPONSIBILITY CRITICISMS

Social responsibility and empirical schools of criticism should try to benefit from each other's works, ideas, and values.

Two ostensibly different schools of criticism can reach roughly the same conclusions. Social responsibility theorists talk in terms that are fairly accessible to everybody, yet they are vulnerable to accusations that only the examples that fit are selected as evidence. Empirical criticisms usually are less vulnerable to charges of a selectivity bias, but may be written in abstract, technical, hard-to-grasp terms. Consider a series of cases in which critics from both schools wound up at roughly the same place.

"THE MISTRESS OR THE MAID?"

Writing for the *Chicago Journalism Review*, author and social critic Studs Terkel (1972) compared the way front-page stories in the *Chicago Tribune* and the *Chicago Sun-Times* covered the news of an armed intruder who had broken into the home of a wealthy industrialist named Henry Crown.

According to the *Tribune*'s version, "A gunman . . . fled empty handed when the maid fought him and Mrs. Crown set off a shrieking burglar alarm." In contrast, the *Sun-Times* offered the following version: "The wife of millionaire industrialist Henry Crown drove an armed intruder from the . . . home . . . after struggling with him and tripping a burglar alarm, police said." In other words, the role of the maid in the *Sun-Times* version was merely that of witness to the heroism and derring-do of her mistress.

Terkel wondered satirically whether the police or the *Tribune* had tried to be "democratic" by inventing the maid's defense of her employer's home and belongings. Despite the differences between the two papers' versions regarding who fought the armed intruder, Terkel noted that the two versions were similar in other ways:

> The maid's name, mentioned once in each story, turns out to be Claramae Santucci. Is it Miss, Mrs. or Ms.? The *Trib* referred to—uh—the being as "the maid" seven times. The *Sun-Times* had her so categorized four times. In both versions every reference to the mistress was "Mrs. Crown."

Terkel said that if the first name, Claramae, meant that the maid was black, he was reminded of black writer James Baldwin's complaint that " 'nobody knows my name.' He was referring to black domestics." If the last name—Santucci—meant the maid was Italian, Terkel concluded, perhaps there *was* a kind of egalitarianism after all: Italian maids get the same shabby treatment as black maids. So at least two explanations seemed possible for this incident: racism and social class bias.

Racism in News?

The *Chicago Journalism Review* has attacked local journalists often for racial prejudice. For example, it pointed out that the *Chicago Daily News* ran two stories on a conference in Chicago on lead poisoning. One story, based on a paper given by a Washington, D.C., veterinarian, told how pets are affected by lead poisoning. It ran

> under a three-deck headline in 48-point: "Lead toxic to puppies in the city." The second paper, presented by an Omaha pediatrician, told of how black children are affected by lead poisoning. The story ran beneath the one about dogs and cats, under a two-line headline in 36-point type: "Blacks prone to lead poisoning."

> After all, *Daily News* readers have more puppies than they have black children [*Chicago Journalism Review*, 1972: 17].

Various *Review* articles have frequently offered the explanation that Chicago journalists are comfortable, middle-class whites who are out of touch with black people:

> Your average everyday American murder . . . is usually dispensed with in three inches of news in the back pages. . . . When black folks kill white

folks we get the full hype and all the grisly details. When the same black
folks kill black folks . . . the media kiss it off [De Zutter, 1972: 12].

Several examples pulled from the news media have almost always
accompanied these generalizations.

Social responsibility-tinged charges of racism aren't limited to the
Chicago Journalism Review. An example from prize-winning investigative journalist Seymour Hirsh, as cited by Pritchard (1985: 500),
relates that when Hirsh was a cub reporter in Chicago, he phoned in
what he thought was a big story: A black man had murdered five people
and then killed himself. The desk man who answered the phone wanted
to know if the five victims were "of the American Negro persuasion."
When Hirsh said they were, the editor told him to "cheapen" (play
down) the story. When it ran, the story was only one or two paragraphs
in the Chicago newspapers.

Noted social responsibility critic Ben Bagdikian (1983: 202) also
contends that the news media downplay news of racial minorities:
"Standard American newspapers and broadcasters would deny that they
are racist. But their policies on reporting the news are indistinguishable
from policies that would deliberately exclude minorities."

To repeat a point made earlier, anecdotal evidence—proof by example—always is vulnerable to the charge that it was selected to fit the
alleged prejudices of the researcher. Since social responsibility critics
very often rely on this kind of evidence, one would think that they
cannot afford to ignore empirical support when it is available. But too
many do.

Earlier in this century, many newspapers were criticized for identifying persons' race in crime stories as "Negro" while not giving the race
of white persons. While the practice has gradually disappeared, as
recently as 1962 a Southern Illinois University sociologist wrote that
"Negro suspects and offenders are identified by race in most Southern
newspapers . . . and . . . in some non-Southern newspapers. . . . A newspaper's race labeling of Negroes (and not of whites) tends to give
an impression" that blacks commit most crimes (quoted in Dulaney,
1969: 603).

After deleting stories in which police were looking for a suspect (and
a physical description, including race, might legitimately be given), and
after also deleting cases in which race seemed to be the motive of the
crime (e.g., a car bombing by three white men outside a civil rights
rally), Dulaney (1969) found only ten cases in his sample of stories in
which the race of the suspect was reported. *In every one of the ten news
stories, however, the race as reported was "Negro" or black.*

In a careful analysis of newspaper coverage of 90 murder arrests and prosecutions in Milwaukee, Pritchard (1985) found that the city's two daily newspapers devoted far less space to coverage of murders when they involved blacks and Hispanics as the alleged *killers* than they did when a white person was accused of the crime. Race of the *victim* did not independently predict the amount of space given. As Pritchard put it, the operative concept in the newsroom seemed to be " 'cheap murderer' rather than 'cheap murder' " when a black or Hispanic was involved. Given the chance to be ruled out as "cause" by other variables, race of the accused killer remained as a powerful predictor of the amount of news space given. This finding provides persuasive support for social responsibility critics, while perhaps redefining and refining the precise nature of the racial bias in crime news.

While it is directly relevant only if one regards sports telecasting as journalism, a study by Rainville and McCormick (1977) is so intriguing that it shouldn't be excluded from this brief sample of studies. Rainville is blind and asserts that he isn't a pro football fan. Nevertheless, he discovered that when he was put in a situation where he had to listen to the audio portion of a televised National Football League game, he was able to identify the race of each player fairly easily. He and McCormick then set out to learn why, using a carefully designed content analysis of NFL telecasts.

They discovered that, for one thing, announcers praised plays by white players more often than they did plays by blacks. Further, blacks were portrayed far more often as the recipients of aggression, while whites were cast as the executors of aggression ("Smith really blasted Jones that time!"). Black players' negative past histories ("Smith is from Oneonta State, where his academic performance kept him off the field for several semesters") were mentioned far more often than were those of white players, and black players far more often suffered in comparison with other players mentioned by announcers ("Jones just doesn't have the speed to keep up with Washington's wide receivers."). Rainville and McCormick concluded that black pro football players were the victims of announcers' "covert" and "unconscious" racial prejudice. (All the announcers in the study were white.)

This study used techniques—such as removing the names of the players from the coding protocols and matching each black with a white player who had roughly equal career achievements—that could readily be transferred to the study of public affairs coverage, and to print as well as broadcast media. One could imagine a similar study, for example, of coverage of Jesse Jackson in 1984 (when reporters may have bent over backward to avoid being critical of the first black candidate for president) with coverage of Jackson as a potential candidate in 1988.

Social Class Discrimination in News?

Studs Terkel's (1972) "The Mistress or the Maid?" raised another question besides race: Are Italian maids treated as badly as black maids? Obviously, this opens up the general issue of whether or not journalists make distinctions based on a person's social class. Little empirical mass communication research has examined the possibility of class-related discrimination by journalists, and relatively little discussion of it can be found in social responsibility-oriented case studies. One partial explanation for the lack of critical attention seems to be that social responsibility-oriented writers would rather not use words like *social class* when they discuss what journalists do.

In perhaps the first empirical study of class bias in the news, Chilton Bush and R. K. Bullock (1952) examined the society pages of two San Francisco Bay Area newspapers. They found a very strong bias toward reporting the social doings of people from upper occupational groups, with almost no attention paid to the social comings and goings of people from lower-status groups. Even Bush and Bullock, however, seemed not to emphasize fully the social class implications of their findings.

However, sociologists don't seem to be as inhibited as journalists and ex-journalists about discussing news practices in class-related terms. In his content analysis of network news and news magazines, sociologist Herbert J. Gans (1980: 23-28) reports that writers avoided paying attention to economic class differences in their stories about events in the United States. In contrast, Gans states, U.S. journalists often report social and economic class conflicts—*in those very terms*—when covering political events in foreign countries. Gans asserts that

> journalists shun the term "working class" because for them it has Marxist connotations, but even non-Marxist notions of class conflict are outside the journalistic repertoire of concepts. Strikes are, of course, reported as conflicts between labor and management; but they . . . are seen as incidents soon to be resolved rather than as permanent conflicts of interest [pp. 24-25].

Unfortunately, Gans provides little by way of documentation of these statements. One can easily imagine a comparison between international and U.S. news treatments of class conflict as virtually a ready-made opportunity to test whether "class conflict" is a nonevent in U.S. news.

(Again, references to class in news about foreign politics would provide the baseline for assessing the hypothetically fewer references in U.S. news.)

Sociologist Warren Breed (1964: 190) also has pointed out that the word *class* simply isn't used when U.S. news media cover social problems, but, again, he provides little documentation to back up his observation.

I don't pretend that this brief sampling of the empirical literature on racism and classism in the news exhausts all the possibilities. Nevertheless, it is clear that, in this case, nonempirical and empirical critics should introduce themselves to each other. After all, they're standing in practically the same place.

COUNTING NOSES (OR WHATEVER)

Reporters routinely estimate the sizes of crowds at political events, or they get police officials to make estimates. One can generally rely on news reports to tell how many people were there, how many balloons there were, or how many people were arrested.

Writing in the *Chicago Journalism Review*, Jane Green (1973: 13) wondered how two of Chicago's newspapers and a radio station could have come up with crowd estimates of 500, 8,000, and 18,000 for the *same* protest march in Chicago's "Loop" area:

> The media generally have a history of poor crowd estimates. . . . Crowd estimates of the September 15 [George] McGovern rally [ranged in Chicago media] . . . from 20,000 to 100,000 people. . . . In 1969, *CJR* compared estimates of a Chicago parade for the astronauts. . . . Using the lesser of the two figures published, one million . . . a crowd of that size would have had to stand 200 people deep all along the parade route, an obvious impossibility.

Of course, the bigger the estimate of the crowd, the happier the event's organizers will be. (Many organizers claim a media bias against them if the numbers are smaller than they "ought" to be. As we'll see next, sometimes it does appear as if editorial policy can bias the estimated size of the crowd.)

Researcher Leon Mann (1974) wanted to see if newspapers' editorial policies affected crowd-size estimates in their news stories. He, too, found enormous variations in the estimated sizes of pro- and anti-Vietnam War rallies from 1965 through 1971. Based on an analysis of newspaper editorials on the war, he classified more than 10 prominent newspapers as prowar and antiwar and examined their reports of crowd estimates for two antiwar rallies in Washington, D.C. For both a 1965 rally and one in 1967, prowar newspapers gave substantially lower war-protest crowd estimates in their news accounts than did antiwar newspapers.

Did newspapers just invent the crowd figures they used? No. In almost all cases, the crowd figures were attributed to somebody—an organizer, a police spokesperson, whatever. In the case of the 1967 rally, two safely "official" estimates were available to, and known by, each newspaper. The Metropolitan Police's crowd estimate was 50,000 to 55,000, while the National Park Police's was 37,000. Most of the antiwar papers used the higher Metro Police estimate, and most of the prowar papers used the lower Park Police figure. If challenged about its estimate, each paper could have used the same defense. Each used an "official" estimate, after all.

THE "SINS OF SEARS"

Probably no social responsibility criticism has been as often made in journalism reviews as the one concerning news media failure to cover stories that should have been covered. Sometimes the explanation critics offer for this failure is incompetence or inertia. But when nonstories involve big advertisers, there would be great embarrassment among journalists if the case could be made convincingly that they failed to cover the story because they didn't wish to offend the advertiser.

The separation of news decisions from the economic self-interest of the media is now a central, consensus value among journalists, thanks in large part to journalists' and journalism educators' gradual acceptance of social responsibility theory. Values such as this one now are so taken for granted that journalism reviews and professional codes of ethics all take it as such an obvious "given" that there's no need to explain or defend it.

Because this value is so well established, any attempt to defend the decision not to do a story is constrained to take the form of a *denial* that there ever was any eye toward the "bottom line." In other words, nobody could afford to admit that he or she decided to avoid offending a powerful economic interest. *Thus the evidence*—and whether or not it can be explained away—*assumes central importance* in cases such as this.

Social responsibility-oriented critics such as Hillier Krieghbaum (1973) tend to rely for their evidence on series of examples or anecdotes. For example, Krieghbaum cites a long series of stories that left out key information, or stories about events of high news value done only by "out of town" news agencies. No matter how many examples a critic strings together, however, he or she is always vulnerable to questions of bias in the selection of those examples: "Okay, so you've given X examples, but how many cases did you have to go through before you could find even this number?"

Further, there are questions of interpretation bias with such examples. Since each example differs in some ways from the others, why or how can the critic interpret them all in the same way? Perhaps the sources for the first story that wasn't run weren't reliable enough, while for the second nonstory the reporter whose responsibility it would have been was swamped with other stories. And so on.

Interpretation bias regarding anecdotal evidence may be a problem that can't be solved completely, as we'll see toward the end of this section. Nevertheless, we can at least ask that the critic supplement clippings or tapes, whenever possible, by asking the responsible journalists why they did it that way. (Once again, however, remember that journalists could not afford to admit that bottom-line considerations were responsible.) Given that journalists have offered *some* reasons for their decisions, social responsibility-oriented critics ought to subject such explanations to certain kinds of tests:

- Are the answers *plausible*? Or does it take a lot of extra faith and trust to believe them?
- Are the answers *consistent*? Or does the journalist contradict what he or she has said somewhere else?
- Are the answers *logical*? Do they really seem to follow from, or lead to, the decision(s) that were made?

Social responsibility critic Michael Hirsh (1976) did ask Chicago reporters to explain why, as the title of his *Columbia Journalism Review* article put it, "the sins of Sears are not news in Chicago." The national headquarters of Sears are housed in a building that dominates the Chicago skyline—as it would dominate any city skyline in the world. Sears employed nearly 30,000 people in Sears Tower and elsewhere in the Chicago area. The Federal Trade Commission accused Sears—the world's largest retailer—of conducting systematic "bait-and-switch" retail scams, in which low-priced products are advertised, but, when the consumer arrives, the products are "out of stock" or "not nearly as good" as a "slightly" higher-priced alternative. Based on the standard criteria of newsworthiness, the story seemed to have had a lot going for it in Chicago news media: It had a very strong local angle, it involved conflict (Sears versus the FTC), and the accusation suggested that some of the millions of Sears customers probably had been victimized.

The trial before a Federal Trade Commission administrative law judge lasted 11 days, at which point Sears abandoned its denials and negotiated for a consent order. The 11 days were packed with testimony against Sears by 18 of its former employees and 25 of its customers. Employees told of such tactics as advertised TV sets deliberately connected to bad antenna systems "so you'd have a bad picture" and advertised sewing machines rigged so that they would rattle when demonstrated to customers.

After hearing the 11 days of testimony, Sears sought the out-of-court settlement. Here's what the Chicago news media did—and did not do—and the explanations they gave Hirsh (1976: 30):

The *Chicago Tribune* "carried not one line about the case from the date the trial began . . . until . . . nearly a week after the trial was halted." When a story finally ran, it was a Dow-Jones News Service report, rather than a local one. That story was four paragraphs long. *Tribune* Managing Editor William M. Jones denied any pressure from Sears not to cover the story. His explanation? "Decisions are made daily as to what stories will be covered, and we chose not to cover that one."

The *Chicago Sun-Times* had a single story midway through the trial plus three stories after the trial ended. The local reporter who wrote two of the posttrial stories said, "There wasn't any resistance to my covering it. . . . It just kept getting shunted aside for other work."

The *Chicago Daily News* ran only two stories. One appeared to be a rewrite of the single *Sun-Times* midtrial story. The other ran after the trial concluded and attributed much of its content to the Dow-Jones News Service. *Daily News* reporter Betty Washington said she checked every day to see who would testify "and found [each day] it was just going to be another salesman from Texas." Also, she said, other trials were going on and she had to cover those, too.

Only two radio stations did any coverage of the trial, each in interview form (a single day for one, two days for the other). There was absolutely no TV news coverage.

This lengthy anecdote started with an assertion that examples as evidence are (1) vulnerable to questions about a bias in selecting only those that suit and (2) vulnerable to alternative explanations. Follow-up interviews with the journalists involved in the decision offered up the hope, at least, that alternative explanations could be ruled out. But did Hirsh manage to do that?

Notice that all three newspaper journalists denied that there was any basis to their decisions other than the fact that the Sears trial wasn't as newsworthy as other things needing to be covered.

Hirsh reported their explanations without comment. Apparently, we, like Hirsh, are expected to see through those explanations. Did he ask them what specific other stories "bumped" the Sears story out of the news almost every day of the trial? We don't know, but we sense that Hirsh simply doesn't believe these journalists' explanations.

Did Hirsh ask reporter Washington why she didn't call the court to get a fill-in on testimony, or why she didn't interview Sears or Federal Trade Commission sources for their accounts of how the trial was going? Surely those would have been rather obvious strategies for a reporter who said she was interested every day in finding out who was going to testify. Instead of sitting in the courtroom, in other words, she could have obtained a summary or recap by telephone—not the best reporting technique, but sometimes necessary for reporters who can be in only one place at a time. We don't know whether Hirsh asked Washington—or any of the others—any of these questions.

The *Tribune*'s Jones seemed to be saying, in effect, "We decided each day what we would cover, and every day we decided not to cover the Sears trial." We didn't because we didn't, in other words. Surely that kind of evasive answer demands a follow-up question, a further probe of some sort. We don't know whether Hirsh asked any further; his article doesn't say.

As any reporter knows, what quotations you use and what you leave out can be a major point of contention. In other words, not only do the specific case studies chosen represent a possible vulnerable area in the evidence given, so do the specific quotations used when the critic asks journalists to explain their decisions. In the Hirsh article, for example, one can ask whether or not the *Tribune, Daily News,* and *Sun-Times* journalists were fully and accurately quoted—for example, is that *all* Jones said, or was only the most evasive-sounding quotation used?

No matter how lengthy the critic's article, or how complete the quotes, ultimately all criticism that relies on evidence by example cannot completely solve such vulnerabilities. That's why empirical evidence should be welcomed by social responsibility-oriented critics as—at the very least—supplementary, supportive evidence from an independent source. In this spirit, consider a classic old study by sociologist Warren Breed, first published in 1958, long before the "Sins of Sears" article.

Earlier, I said that empirical researchers have developed a number of ways of discovering what does *not* appear in the news. Breed's study was one of the first. A former newspaperman and a Ph.D. graduate of Columbia University's Department of Sociology, Breed did the pioneering study of what the news media kept out of the news. He conducted what he termed a "reverse content analysis" by compiling lists of topics that did not appear in the news media. Breed based his list of topics on (1) the issues and problems mentioned in 11 classic sociological studies of American communities, (2) topics mentioned to him by newspaper journalists as excluded from their own newspapers, and (3) a book of cartoons that had been rejected by popular publications.

Breed said he found some 250 topics—presumably each of them newsworthy by ordinary criteria—that were not covered by local news media. About two-thirds of these topics, he reported, concerned advantages granted or taken by economic interests "in a nondemocratic" way. Examples cited from the community studies included how a city railroad grade crossing construction project was abandoned when manufacturers found it would disturb their loading operations, how a private power and light company was allowed to continue a smoke nuisance, how employers inserted anti-social security literature into their workers' pay envelopes, and so on. Presumably, the "Sins of Sears" case would fall into this large category that Breed called "politicoeconomic" topics.

After politicoeconomic topics, religion was the next most common topic excluded from the news, but religion involved only about 20% of the total. Examples of "religious" topics kept out of the news included rivalries among churches in the community and the trend toward nonreligious activities (e.g., bingo games as fund raisers) at church functions. Following religion, items concerning the justice system and doctors and hospitals were most commonly excluded, Breed reported.

Empirical researchers are becoming increasingly clever at creating ways to document things that do *not* appear in the news, in contrast to things that do. Breed's approach seems fairly primitive today.

LABOR IN THE NEWS

As mentioned earlier in this chapter, social responsibility-oriented critics are concerned about such perceived media failures as a lack of news about threats to workers posed by their work environments.

However, such discussions generally aren't cast into "working-class" or similar terms. Sometimes, the critic mentions briefly that journalists aren't blue-collar workers, probably aren't union members, and come from relatively well-educated, white-collar professional backgrounds—implying, in other words, that individual reporters therefore have trouble identifying with blue-collar workers.

Communication researchers Douglas et al. (1985) analyzed coverage of worker-related issues in three middle-sized Illinois dailies. These researchers found far more attention paid to issues such as strikes than to occupational health and safety matters or other issues relating to how the employer affected workers. Furthermore, even when the papers covered employer actions affecting workers, "there was an overemphasis on the actions of public sector employers" (p. 859) rather than the much larger number of private sector employers. "Employers' application of technology to the processes of production and distribution—and the consequences it has for the labor force and the nature of work—did not seem to be within the frame of reference of these dailies" (p. 860). Noting that earlier studies of radio network and TV network coverage also had found "distorted" and "unfair" portraits of workers and unions, Douglas et al. conclude that "there has been no appreciable change over several decades in the way media characterize these matters" (p. 860).

Why would the actions of public employers receive more emphasis than those of private sector employers? First, the news media tacitly treat the actions of government as everybody's business, but the actions of private sector management as, at most, grist for the business pages—unless something highly unusual or dramatic transforms "private" action into a public concern. Second, government actions affecting employees tend to have specific decision times and places that public affairs reporters can easily mark. In contrast, conditions in the private workplace often are determined by a series of low-profile, unannounced decisions—not at all easy to notice when most reporters are not assigned to the "private sector" anyhow.

Douglas et al. report that the single most common setting for a story about work and labor—about a third of all labor-related news stories—was a union-called strike or other job action. That statistic alone suggests a great distortion in news media coverage of work and labor, since more than four of every five American workers are *not* unionized. The proportion of nonunion workers has been growing steadily since just after World War II. Given the weakening of unions as speakers for labor, one would think that American news media would be searching for new ways to cover the single most common daily activity of adult Americans—work.

A CHICANO STRIKE IN TEXAS

Given the importance of the strike as a "hard news" event, we might have expected a great deal of news coverage when Chicano workers struck the Economy Furniture Factory in Austin, Texas. The National Labor Relations Board had certified as accurate the workers' election of the Upholsterer's International Union as their collective bargaining agent. Some six months after company management refused to recognize the election results, workers began what turned out to be a 2-year strike. (Most of the information presented here about this strike comes from a fascinating social responsibility-tinged narrative case study by Rada, 1977.)

During the first year of the strike, coverage of it—and of the union's complaints about management's refusal to negotiate—was virtually nonexistent in Texas news media. The union decided to commemorate the first anniversary of the strike by marching to the steps of the State Capitol in Austin. When the City of Austin suddenly withdrew a parade permit it had granted, the union marched anyway, setting up the classic scenario that groups without access seem to need to compel news coverage: Would the Austin police stop the march? If so, would they use tear gas? News media that previously wouldn't cover the dispute between the union and Economy Furniture now were out in force, covering The Confrontation. Television footage and photos emphasized the lines of rigid police—tear gas containers and billy clubs at the ready—as the marchers peacefully walked past. There were no arrests, and the march was completed.

In the characteristic pattern of media coverage, the march was covered as a "public disturbance." There was no coverage of what speakers said on the Capitol steps, so there was almost no information in the media about why the marchers marched and what their disputes were with the company. (The same journalistic pattern of screening out the substantive reasons for demonstrations occurred during coverage of anti-Vietnam War demonstrations; see Gitlin, 1980.)

The union, after observing the coverage of its first anniversary march, did something very unusual: It complained to the Federal Communications Commission about what broadcasters screened out, sending carbon copies of the complaint to the news media. After receiving copies of the complaint, television and even newspaper newspeople suddenly were contacting the union to get its side of the story.

On the second anniversary, the union conducted a similar march and rally. This time, a parade permit was granted, lowering the conflict level. For this occasion, however, the union had invited a spokesman who couldn't easily be ignored, famed California farm-labor organizer Cesar Chavez. Television covered the parade and rally, interviewing union leaders as well. "The electronic media seemed almost eager to please" (Rada, 1977: 112). Eventually, the company, which was also being hurt by a union-organized boycott of its furniture products, agreed to abide by a court order to negotiate.

The major lesson Rada draws from his case study is that, "of necessity, [civil rights and other social action groups] have resorted to staging events and breaking laws to manipulate and coerce local media into providing coverage of unpopular issues" (p. 113).

At various points already in this book, we have seen empirical documentation of a fundamental problem in modern American journalism: its insensitivity and inaccessibility to calm, reasoned, and rational arguments made by sources who lack "credentials." You will recall that news objectivity has come to mean both that

> all opinions in the news must be attributed to a "source" and
>
> the more official and obvious the source is, the fewer questions there can be about the selection of both the opinion statements and the source; and, therefore,
>
> once the above two "requirements" for objectivity are met, the reporter can be perfectly, safely objective merely by assuring the accuracy of the statements attributed to the source.

Sources lacking access to make their case in the news thus are confronted with the situation Rada characterizes as a "necessity"—the resort to staged confrontations and lawbreaking. However, these tactics produce a dilemma. While access to the media may, indeed, be "coerced" by staging such events, what kind of news coverage results? If you are covered as a disturbance to the peace, a rabble-rouser, and lawbreaker, how is that coverage going to help you make your case? That such coverage will result is extremely predictable. Turning a liability into an asset, the union turned this predictable outcome to its own advantage by complaining to the FCC. But if the FCC continues to "deregulate" broadcasting, can one be sure that a complaint to the FCC will continue to cause nervous shudders among station managers? If the only result of compelling coverage is to transform what one says into a series of affronts and provocations in the eyes of the mass public, has one really gained anything?

The obvious solution is to create in journalists an awareness of how they are unintentionally teaching sources without credentials to distort their rhetoric and tactics in order to "compel" access. Journalists need to rethink what it means to be "objective" in news about public affairs. As hard as it will be to persuade them to do this, the social cost of getting journalists to change will be far smaller than the social costs we've already incurred because "uncredentialed" leaders of social movements can gain news attention only by drastically changing what they have to say.

"THE SAME OLD MISTAKES"

Former NBC correspondent and Ford administration press secretary Ron Nessen complained in a 1979 *Newsweek* column that, in spite of themselves, journalists keep making the same mistakes when they cover presidential campaigns. Political scientist and newspaper editor Edwin Diamond (1980: 19) asserted in the *Washington Journalism Review*:

> The campaign press corps is made up of a group of basically decent, hard-working, intelligent men and women who are sincere about their work—and *institutionally unable to cover election campaigns properly* [emphasis added].

Nessen and Diamond, like many social responsibility-oriented critics, assert that the news media commit several blunders every time they cover the presidential primary and fall campaigns:

- They fail to provide enough information about candidates' policy positions.
- They fail to provide equal access to news coverage for all the contenders during the primaries.
- They treat the campaign as a "horse race," trivializing it.
- They place far too much importance on the New Hampshire primary and begin to rule candidates out on the basis of it.

Once again, a variety of empirical evidence supports these criticisms.

In an earlier study, I found that both before and after the New Hampshire primary, network news clearly was concentrating on certain candidates' campaigns and virtually ignoring those of others (Lemert, 1981). Furthermore, drastic discrepancies in how often candidates' names were mentioned in the news were making dramatic differences in voters' ability to recall the names of those candidates. This name-familiarity effect, in turn, could be expected to influence how candidates stood in the polls. Standings in the polls, in turn, could be expected to widen discrepancies in how often the media mentioned candidates' names. I also found that Carter's 1976 "victory" in New Hampshire actually had boosted Morris Udall's campaign more than Carter's, at least among samples of Oregon voters and Democratic Central Committee members. Meanwhile, Oregon journalists who were key gatekeepers of political news in the state's major media were rapidly deciding, less than a week after New Hampshire, that Carter clearly was the most newsworthy candidate, since he was the likely nominee.

Robinson (1978) reports that his 1976 content analysis of newspaper news coverage found that twice as many stories were broadcast about New Hampshire as about any of the next seven primaries. In 1980, the amount of news coverage given the New Hampshire primary (with only a third as many delegates at stake as in Minnesota) completely outstripped the amount of coverage given the Minnesota precinct caucuses, which were held on the same day as the New Hampshire primary (Joslyn, 1984).

What about the "horse race" criticism? (Reporting on the polls and on a candidate's tactics, financial resources, and strategic plans all would be examples of horse race coverage.) If the news media do emphasize the horse race aspect during the primaries and after the summer nominating conventions, we would expect such coverage to be at the expense of two types of information that "rational" voters would want to have before casting a ballot: (1) the policy positions of the candidates, and (2) the personal qualifications of the candidates. Following is a sampling of the empirical evidence.

Policy information. Graber (1980) reports that horse race coverage far outstripped policy coverage in 1968, 1972, and 1976, and the discrepancy grew larger over the years. Newspapers were about as likely as TV news to provide more horse race than policy coverage. Joslyn (1984: 145) concludes that, even when there was coverage of policy positions, the news media selected only some policies to cover: "issues that neatly divide candidates, produce disagreement and argument among candidates, and can be summarized with simple slogans."

Patterson (1980) found that half of newspaper and magazine content devoted to coverage of candidates' issue positions focused on such simple, clean-cut issues, and two-thirds of network news issue coverage did.

Oregon graduate student Alan Abbey (1977) reports that major political columnists gave even less issue coverage when they wrote about the televised presidential debates in 1976 than they did in 1960.

Patterson and McClure's 1972 campaign survey results showed that voters actually learned more about McGovern's and Nixon's policy views from televised political ads than they did from the network news. These results were bolstered by the two authors' content analysis of issue coverage in the campaign (Patterson and McClure, 1976). In fairness, however, I should mention that Zhao and Chaffee (1986) found that 1984 voters seemed to learn more about candidates' policy views from TV news coverage of the Reagan-Mondale campaigns than they did from broadcast political ads. But even Zhao and Chaffee's survey results don't say much about whether TV news *content* provides "enough" issue information to voters (however *enough* is defined).

Candidate qualifications. Patterson and McClure (1976) found that each network gave from 5 to 15 minutes' coverage during the entire fall campaign to Richard Nixon's qualifications; McGovern's qualifications received from 3 to 7 minutes. Those are total times, from Labor Day to the November election! ("Qualifications" included experience, health, personality traits, and the like.)

In recent years, few topics have received as much attention as the way journalists do (and do not) cover what's going on in national election campaigns. The empirical evidence provides strong support for what social responsibility theorists say are the failures of all the news media to provide an adequate information base for voters. In addition, the evidence suggests that the news media, by prematurely defining candidates as "no-hopers," create circumstances that lead to the elimination of candidates before voters even know their names. (See especially Lemert, 1981.)

What may be more interesting than the agreement between social responsibility and empirical critics about what is wrong with campaign coverage is the sometimes sharp discrepancy between the two schools in the depth of their *causal analysis* of these failings. Nessen (1979) and Diamond (1980) merely remarked, respectively, that journalists vowed not to repeat errors of the past—and then did—and that the problem was with the "news institution" itself, not with the individual journalists. Well, what did Diamond mean by the "news institution"? The only hint Diamond gives us about institutional causes of the problem is a vague reference to deadline pressures.

If critics really want to change the way journalists cover presidential elections, they'll have to do a better job of identifying the forces that seem to compel such practices as overemphasis of the New Hampshire primary and premature elimination of candidates who don't do well in the first one or two primaries.

In contrast to these two fairly representative social responsibility-oriented critics, empirically oriented researchers and theorists provide a body of literature now that offers considerable insight into why journalists seem to keep doing the same terrible things every four years. Perhaps the most penetrating institutional analysis has been that of political scientist Chris Arterton (1978) in a paper prepared for the American Assembly, a group that was to make a number of proposals about changes, both in journalism and in the presidential primary election system. Let me offer a composite summary that brings together Arterton's findings, my own work, and that by others in explaining why it is extremely difficult for journalists, unaided, to change the way they cover the primaries.

Why Horse Race Coverage?

Powerful incentives are built into the business and prestige structures of the media that concentrate journalistic resources on finding out who is going to win. Reporters who can accurately predict how the next primary is going to turn out impress the heck out of the "boys on the bus" (Crouse, 1974). The sooner the home office can learn definitively who hasn't got a chance, the more money it can save by pulling camera crews and reporters away from covering that candidate. Those people then can be reassigned by a short-staffed home office to cover other stories. Traditionally, a journalist is assigned to cover only one candidate. If that candidate makes it to the White House, that journalist has gained a top assignment for at least the next four years. Therefore, ambitious and competitive journalists have vested interests in being assigned to the candidate with the best chance, so they'll continually assess how "their" candidate is doing in the horse race. If the journalist and the home office can learn, more quickly than the campaign organization itself does, that this candidate has a "lock" on the nomination, then the journalist has a chance to make the extra effort to establish good contacts with sources inside the campaign. If the campaign organization learns that it has a lock before the journalist does, the journalist will find that the campaign organization suddenly has become very distant and unapproachable except through designated spokespeople.

If all the above institutional factors weren't enough to produce news media fascination with how well each candidate is doing, political journalists (who are the ones covering these elections) tend themselves to be "campaign junkies" who are vicariously "running" the campaign of "their" candidates, secretly tabulating the mistakes.

Why Overemphasize New Hampshire?

Actually, the same question could be asked as well about the Iowa caucuses and "straw poll" ballots taken a year or two before the primaries even begin. Journalists begin anticipating the next presidential election almost the day after the last one. For example, news media speculation about George Bush's prospects for the 1988 Republican nomination began over the air and in print the day the 1984 election results were known. After literally years of speculation, polls, and straw polls, New Hampshire (and the Iowa caucus preceding it) have become landmark "hard news" events, the first really definitive measures of how the contenders are doing. With New Hampshire and Iowa, then, journalists think they finally have definitive news to work with.

This is not to say that polls, speculations, and media-created tests of candidates' "viability" aren't used before New Hampshire to make tentative judgments about who is—and isn't—viable as a candidate. For example, journalists tend to regard as a key preprimary test of viability whether or not a candidate has raised enough money in the required 20 different states to qualify for federal matching funds for the primary campaign. Even though there is no legal requirement to raise the money that soon in 20 different states, candidates find themselves under extreme pressure from journalists to establish their legitimacy as "viable" presidential candidates. By the summer of 1975, for example, 1976 candidate Terry Sanford's staff reported "being told specifically [by journalists] they would not be covered until they had qualified [for federal matching funds]" (Arterton, 1978: 14).

Behind the scenes, then, many months before the primaries have begun, journalists are willing to tell campaign staffers who they think is a viable candidate—and who isn't. (These expectations have often been embarrassingly wrong, by the way.)

But at least one senses that journalists' hints about who has a chance—and who hasn't—are tentative and relatively low key *when in news reports* prior to the New Hampshire primary. After the "official" New Hampshire election results begin to come in, however, those definitions of winners and losers harden up considerably. In the 1976 campaign, for example, CBS already was declaring Birch Bayh, Fred

Harris, and Sargeant Shriver "washed up" exactly one week after the New Hampshire primary (see Lemert, 1981: 63-81).

Correspondents for the networks need to "sell" their stories to editors back at their home offices. They realize that each evening's newscast will carry fewer than 20 stories, and that the presidential primaries' share of those few stories doesn't rise sharply as the number of contending candidates rises. As a result, correspondents are under pressure to read significance and portent into the most trivial of early campaign day-to-day developments in order to "make it" onto that night's newscast. Competition for space is almost as severe among correspondents covering individual candidates for the major newspapers. The longer the reporter is away from the home office—and thus cut off from other forms of feedback—the more important "making it" onto the newscast or the front page can be as reassurance that editors are satisfied.

Why Journalists Don't Cover Policy Issues

As we've seen, horse race coverage seems to occur at the expense of reporting candidates' policy views. We cannot trust journalism to correct itself here for several reasons.

First, network news decision makers seem to believe that their audiences aren't interested in substantive, serious coverage of policy disputes (see Patterson and McClure, 1976: 143-156). If anything, the trend away from issue coverage may be growing more extreme on network news (Graber, 1980).

Second, political reporters have both more interest and more experience in covering the nuts and bolts of campaigns than they do in covering substantive policy issues.

Third, the subject matter expertise of political reporters is politics— not economics, foreign policy, or whatever else candidates are talking about. Since a reporter is assigned to cover only one candidate's campaign, there's relatively little chance for him or her to do the homework of asking for substantive rebuttals from experts provided by the opposing campaign(s).

Fourth, any effort to bring in reporters who do have policy expertise probably would be met with great resistance by the dominant political journalists. In 1980, for instance, ABC's economics specialist, Dan Cordtz, was among many economics reporters who complained that their requests to cover candidates' economics-related policy positions were met with hostility and foot-dragging in the newsroom, despite the fact that polls showed the economy to be the primary voting issue in 1980. The polls also showed that audiences wanted more information about candidates' economic policies. The institution of the news "beat" also can be thought of as a fence-line that marks areas of exclusivity. In journalism, you cross that line onto someone else's "turf" at your peril.

Fifth, political correspondents are under severe institutional pressure to justify the expense of keeping them in the field. Cut off for extended periods from much editorial feedback, reporters quickly learn that the editors back home are checking their campaign reports against those provided by the Associated Press and other news services. Submitting a story that strays too far from the herd can lead to static from the home office. As we've seen, straightforward coverage of a candidate's policy views definitely would mark the correspondent as a stray.

Sixth, and finally, issue coverage has a hard time becoming part of campaign news because reporters have heard the candidate make the same policy speeches so many times that they literally can complete each line before the speaker does. (This, of course, does not explain why, even when they hear The Speech for the first time, reporters fail to cover its substantive content.) If The Speech is "nothing new" to the reporter, there's a natural leap to the false conclusion that the content of The Speech wouldn't be news, either, to the reporter's audience. Research clearly shows that most Americans don't even become interested in presidential campaigns until quite late—long after reporters have heard The Speech many times (see, e.g., Lemert et al., 1983). Therefore, even if reporters covered the policy statement the first time they heard it, most of the audience wouldn't have paid attention to the story. Later in the campaign, when the audience is interested, they *would* attend to that story (Lemert et al., 1983). The Speech, therefore, *is* news to the audience, as anyone who stands in a typical crowd late in the primary season can attest: Many in the crowd respond to The Speech as if they are hearing it for the first time, because they are!

Why Deny Access Prematurely?

Reporters, producers, and camera operators are expensive. As we've already seen, news media are under pressure to pull back staffers quickly from candidates perceived to have no prospects. So far, at least, a kind of stripped-down "deathwatch" crew is assigned to cover each candidate, at least until New Hampshire, though already the candidate who is not perceived as a front-runner has almost no chance of being mentioned as often as the front-runners (Lemert, 1981).

Decisions by national news media about which candidacies are moribund will strongly influence news decisions by journalists elsewhere in the United States, judging by a study of how Oregon political editors and reporters reacted to national coverage of the 1976 New Hampshire primary (Lemert, 1981). Oregon journalists seemed tentatively to be planning to "budget" staff resources only to the frontrunners (as defined by the national media) when they came to Oregon for its primary.

Candidates' standings in the polls—measured long before most Americans even know many of their names—also help lead to premature decisions to ration space and time. Thus a kind of self-fulfilling system is set up: Lacking name familiarity, "new" candidates don't show well in the polls. Not showing well in the polls means that they don't get much news coverage, which, in turn, is justified by their low standing in the polls.

At present, the only clear ways for a candidate to overcome this vicious circle of access and name familiarity are to have enough advertising money to buy name familiarity or to put most of the campaign's remaining resources into the New Hampshire primary—and hope for the best. The advertising gambit, however, is severely constrained because of federal matching fund restrictions on campaign spending during the primaries. Eugene McCarthy, George McGovern, Jimmy Carter, and Gary Hart all have demonstrated how a "surprise" showing in New Hampshire can be used to persuade journalists to treat one's campaign seriously. The question, however, then becomes: What if the candidate, for one reason or another, doesn't appeal to New Hampshire voters? Is New Hampshire really enough like the rest of the country to predict how that candidate would do everywhere else?

Solutions: Can Journalism Change Itself?

As Nessen's column suggests, many journalists are well aware that the news media fail to do an adequate job of covering presidential elections. The fact that these failures are repeated every four years with numbing regularity, however, suggests, at the very least, that the problem can't be solved by individuals. The problem is built into the news media as institutions. Of the solutions that have been suggested, those offering the best hope, in my opinion, involve changes in the primary election system. Some changes in journalistic coverage of presidential elections would follow as news institutions adapted to such election system changes.

Shortening and compressing the primary election season would conserve campaign funds so that candidates would have more money available to buy access to voters in more states through advertising on stations whose signals cover several states. More important, if multiple primaries were held on each of (say) only four permissible dates, more candidates might be able to claim a victory in at least one state—and thus journalists would be less able to justify ignoring so many of them after the first month's primary elections. Scheduling four "super primary" dates also might make it easier for the commercial networks to justify to themselves the broadcasting of candidate debates before each of these four dates. So, even if reporters never report the policy views of candidates, voters would have a better chance of learning what those views are through such debates. Lemert et al. (1983) report that watching a televised New Hampshire primary debate created voter interest that wouldn't have been there otherwise, and led to further learning about the campaign.

In recent years, several bills to shorten and compress the primary election system have been introduced in Congress. Even without such legislation, we are starting to see politicians groping toward an alternative primary system that might work, such as the 1988 southern "super primary." It will be instructive to observe whether the existence of even one such multistate "super primary" day causes a shift of attention away from New Hampshire and a delay in pronouncing the death of certain candidacies.

SUMMARY

This chapter has described a series of extended illustrations of how social responsibility-oriented and empirical critics can supplement and support each other. These illustrations covered the convergence of the two critical schools in each of the following areas: racism and social class bias in the news, how journalists count crowds, what kinds of stories seem not to be reported, whether or not labor gets an even break in the news, and a series of problems in the way the news media cover election campaigns. While this chapter stressed convergences among social responsibility and empirical criticisms, the same synergism is, in principle, possible between and among all four schools of criticism.

The next chapter explores the empirical research process by helping the reader to imagine having to make the hard choices researchers have made. How else could they have tested that? Deciding to do it in that way, what did they give up, and what did they gain?

REFERENCES

ABBEY, A. (1977) "Newspaper columnist coverage of the 1960 and 1976 'Great Debates.'" M.A. thesis, University of Oregon School of Journalism.

ARTERTON, F. C. (1978) "Campaign organizations confront the media-political environment," pp. 3-25 in J. D. Barber (ed.) Race for the Presidency: The Media and the Nominating Process. Englewood Cliffs, NJ: Prentice-Hall.

BAGDIKIAN, B. H. (1983) The Media Monopoly. Boston: Beacon.

BREED, W. (1964) "Mass communication and sociocultural integration," pp. 183-200 in L. A. Dexter and D. M. White (eds.) People, Society, and Mass Communications. New York: Free Press.

BUSH, C. R. and R. K. BULLOCK (1952) "Names in the news: a study of two dailies." Journalism Quarterly 29 (Spring): 148-157.

Chicago Journalism Review (1972) "Tidbits." Vol. 5 (December): 17.

CLARKE, P. and S. H. EVANS (1983) Covering Campaigns: Journalism in Congressional Elections. Stanford, CA: Stanford University Press.

Commission on Freedom of the Press (1947) A Free and Responsible Press. Chicago: University of Chicago Press.

CROUSE, T. (1974) The Boys on the Bus. New York: Ballantine.

DE ZUTTER, H. D. (1972) "De newsboy nation: four competing gangs of urban terrorists." Chicago Journalism Review 5 (December): 11-12.

DIAMOND, E. (1980) "Shooting the wounded." Washington Journalism Review 2 (November): 19.

DOUGLAS, S., N. PECORA, and T. GUBACK (1985) "Work, workers and the workplace: is local newspaper coverage adequate?" Journalism Quarterly 62: 855-860.

DULANEY, W. L. (1969) "Identification of race in newspaper crime stories." Journalism Quarterly 46 (Autumn): 603-605.

GANS, H. J. (1980) Deciding What's News: A Study of CBS Evening News, NBC Nightly News, Newsweek and Time. New York: Vintage.

GITLIN, T. (1980) The Whole World Is Watching: Mass Media in the Making and Unmaking of the New Left. Berkeley: University of California Press.

GRABER, D. (1980) Mass Media and American Politics. Washington, DC: Congressional Quarterly Press.

GREEN, J. (1973) "Crowds, crowds, crowds, crowds." Chicago Journalism Review 5 (March): 13.

HIRSH, M. (1976) "The sins of Sears are not news in Chicago." Columbia Journalism Review 15 (July/August): 29-30.

JOSLYN, R. (1984) Mass Media and Elections. Reading, MA: Addison-Wesley.

KRIEGHBAUM, H. (1973) Pressures on the Press. New York: Crowell.

LEMERT, J. B. (1981) Does Mass Communication Change Public Opinion After All? Chicago: Nelson-Hall.

LEMERT, J. B., W. ELLIOTT, K. NESTVOLD, and G. R. RARICK (1983) "Effects of viewing a presidential primary debate: an experiment." Communication Research 10 (April): 155-173.

MANN, L. (1974) "Counting the crowd: effects of editorial policy on estimates." Journalism Quarterly 51 (Summer): 278-285.

NESSEN, R. (1979) "The same old mistakes." Newsweek (November 5): 29.

PATTERSON, T. E. (1980) The Mass Media Election: How Americans Choose Their President. New York: Praeger.

PATTERSON, T. E. and R. D. McCLURE (1976) The Unseeing Eye: The Myth of Television Power in National Elections. New York: G. P. Putnam's Sons.

PRITCHARD, D. (1985) "Race, homicide and newspapers." Journalism Quarterly 62 (Autumn): 500-507.

RADA, S. F. (1977) "Manipulating the media: a case study of a Chicano strike in Texas." Journalism Quarterly 54 (Fall): 109-113.

RAINVILLE, R. E. and E. McCORMICK (1977) "Extent of covert racial prejudice in pro football announcers' speech." Journalism Quarterly 54 (Spring): 20-26.

ROBINSON, M. J. (1978) "TV's newest program: the presidential nominations game." Public Opinion 1 (May-June): 41-46.

SUSSMANN, L. A. (1945) "Labor in the radio news: an analysis of content." Journalism Quarterly 22 (September): 207-214.

TERKEL, S. (1972) "The mistress or the maid?" Chicago Journalism Review 4 (February): 19.

TUCHMAN, G. (1978) Making News: A Study in the Construction of Reality. New York: Free Press.

WEAVER, D. H. and G. C. WILHOIT (1986) The American Journalist: A Portrait of U.S. News People and Their Work. Bloomington: Indiana University Press.

ZHAO, X. and S. H. CHAFFEE (1986) "Political ads vs. news as sources of issue information." Presented to the Communication Theory and Methodology Division at the annual meeting of the Association for Education in Journalism and Mass Communication, Norman, OK.

6

DOING EMPIRICAL CRITICISM OF MEDIA PERFORMANCE

The art of doing empirical criticisms often first means deciding what choices to make.

Going further into the critical research process, we can put ourselves into the shoes of the empirical critic who is planning a study, emphasizing the choices and trade-offs the researcher makes. We'll do this by looking closely at studies done in each of several topic areas:

(1) the effects of chain ownership on newspapers' editorial vigor

(2) "Afghanistanism" in the coverage of environmental problems

(3) the way newspapers cover news of the crime of rape

(4) "whodunit" (Did journalists withhold mobilizing information from news of controversy, or did sources withhold mobilizing information from journalists?)

(5) the "official source syndrome"

EFFECTS OF CHAIN OWNERSHIP

We've already heard about the social responsibility-based complaint that chain ownership of newspapers means that subscribers get lower-quality newspapers. But, even if we were able to do the most complete content analysis ever done of what chain-owned newspapers now give readers, what would we have proven? Suppose, for example, that we could establish that one-third of all their news stories were written by local staff. Is that figure too high, too low, or about right? Suppose, as well, that we showed that 30% of all the editorials in chain-owned daily newspapers concerned local events or issues. Again, is that percentage high, low, or about right?

The question that needs to be asked of these numbers is, Compared to what? As covered in Chapter 4, making things into variables allows us to create baselines for comparison. Thus making chain ownership one *value* of an "ownership" variable will allow us to compare these numbers against those for other newspapers that are *not* chain-owned.

"Time" as Another Variable

Comparing independently owned newspapers and those owned by chains or groups (like Times-Mirror or Gannett), however, might not prove as much as we'd like. Many chains say that they don't meddle with their newly acquired newspapers' editorial policies, often keeping the same managements in place. But what if the kind of newspaper most likely to be acquired by a chain is vulnerable to acquisition because it *already* doesn't have a strong local news staff, or *already* doesn't project a strong editorial voice in the community? So, if we found less local news coverage or less vigorous editorializing in chain-owned newspapers, we have to consider the possibility that the newspapers were already that way when the chains acquired them.

To rule out that possibility, it is necessary to do *another* comparison: Does local news coverage or editorial vigor drop off after the newspaper has been acquired by a chain? One way to answer this is to compare the content of the newspaper while it was independent against the content after it had become part of a chain or group. This comparison can be built in as a "time" variable in a classic "before-after" research design. "Before" is one value of the time variable, and "after" is the other. Before-after designs also allow us to use the "same" newspaper and the "same" city. Presumably, any differences between the before and after measures are due to the change in ownership, not to other factors. So far, the study design is as depicted in Table 6.1.

We've said that we need, for comparison, a group of still-independent newspapers. Few American cities have more than one newspaper, and even fewer have fully competitive newspapers. This means that whatever group of independent newspapers we choose in the after period will almost certainly not be located in the same cities as the newly chain-owned ones. We may have a problem, then, if the independents' cities are somehow politically more cantankerous and dispute-ridden than the chain newspapers' cities. This potential problem can be minimized by also getting a before measure for the still-independents. The study design now looks like Table 6.2.

This design allows us to determine more precisely whether or not any difference between the two groups in the after period results from the differences between their cities. Presumably, any after differences between the two groups of cities would *also* show up in the before

TABLE 6.1

Before	*After*
Initially independent newspapers	Same newspapers, now chain-owned
	Comparison group of independents

measures, *if* newspaper content merely reflects differences between the two groups of cities.

The design shown in Table 6.2 also helps solve another possible problem. Suppose changes are taking place in the entire newspaper industry, such as the movement toward one-newspaper towns. Will that produce changes in newspaper content, regardless of whether a paper is independent or chain-owned? For example, perhaps monopoly newspapers tend to play it safe, trying not to offend or arouse powerful interest groups that could start rival newspapers. If something like this happens, we might find, over time, the vigor of editorials falling—even among the independents. Arguably, of course, the reverse also could happen: Secure in their near-monopoly situation, *all* newspapers might now editorialize more vigorously—regardless of whether or not they are owned by chains. Having both before and after measures for the still-independent newspapers thus protects us against confusing industrywide trends with changes in the content of the newly "chained" newspapers.

So, now we have the basic design: before and after measures for each group of newspapers. University of Oregon graduate student Ralph Thrift (1977) still had a number of tough choices to make before he could do this study, however. His next decision was how to select the newspapers for study.

Choosing the Newspapers

Most, but by no means all, of the roughly 1,700 daily newspapers in the United States are owned by chains. Given the large number of newspapers that could be studied, it was clear from the outset that Thrift needed to draw a *sample* of them. Using random (chance-determined selection) sampling, he drew sample issues of sixteen formerly independent newspapers that had been bought by chains and of eight that had remained independent.

TABLE 6.2

Before	Purchase by Chain?	After
Initially independent	Yes	Same newspapers, now chain-owned
Independent newspapers	No	Still independent

Thrift built several additional refinements into his sample. He wanted to make sure that his two groups of newspapers were *matched* by circulation so that content differences between them couldn't be due to differences in their circulations. (We know that circulation is roughly proportional to the size of a newspaper's news and editorial staff.) To eliminate circulation differences, Thrift made sure that his two groups of newspapers had exactly the same proportion of newspapers in each of four different circulation-size groups. One-fourth of his chain-purchased newspapers came from each circulation group, as did one-fourth of his independent newspapers. We call this a *stratified* sample—this particular stratification ensures that equal proportions come from each circulation group. One can also think of this as similar to what experimenters call "matching." Matching by circulation made possible comparisons between the two types of newspapers *within* each of the four circulation groups, if necessary. Since there were four circulation groups, there were four newly purchased dailies in each to compare against the two independent dailies.

Why did Thrift choose twice as many chain-purchased newspapers as still-independent ones? His principal interest was in whether the chain newspapers changed after purchase by the chain. The eight still-independent newspapers were to provide a baseline against which the sixteen chain newspapers were to be compared. The more chain-owned newspapers in the sample, the greater the chance of spotting any unusual discrepancies among them.

Thrift had to make one more hard choice in setting up his sample: Given his resources, he decided to sample only from a population of West Coast newspapers. The risk in this decision, of course, was that perhaps his results wouldn't be generalizable to other regions. However, if he found differences between chain papers and independents *after*—but *not* before—the purchase, *this difference could not be due to the fact that all were West Coast newspapers*, since the West Coast location was a constant. (For the purposes of argument, assume that the effects of chain ownership differ depending on what section of the country the newspaper is in. Had Thrift pulled his sample from the entire country, it would have been almost inevitable—given the laws of random selection—that at least one of his four circulation groups would have had a regional mismatch in it, with the chain newspapers coming from one region and the independents from another. This would have created a situation in which we couldn't know for sure whether an unexpected result was specific to that circulation group or due to the regional mismatch.)

Choosing the Content

More hard choices faced the researcher here. Given limited resources, Thrift couldn't study both editorials and news content. He chose editorials, justifying his choice with the argument that newspapers regard their editorial page as their prized "heart and soul" (Oakes, 1968: 2). As such, editorials should serve as a sensitive indicator of changes caused by new ownership. We could add a second justification here: Many newspaper chains assert that they don't interfere with their newspapers' editorial policies. A study of editorials allows us to compare rhetoric with empirical result.

How many editorials should be content-analyzed for each newspaper? Thrift chose to examine all editorials in 18 issues of each newspaper during each of the study periods (before and after). Newspapers vary a great deal in how many editorials they run each day, but 18 issues most likely would generate a statistically reliable number, even among smaller newspapers. Thrift structured his random sample of 18 issues so that all issues were published on exactly the same days for chain and independent newspapers within each circulation stratum (so days became a constant).

If the time period were to be the same for all the newspapers in a given circulation group, Thrift decided, it should be long enough *before* the chain's purchase for the formerly independent newspapers to be as vigorous and "healthy" as they normally had been: The closer to the time of purchase, the greater the chances that management was looking to sell an already weakened paper. Using this reasoning, Thrift decided to sample each formerly independent newspaper a minimum of three years prior to its purchase. To accomplish this, he made his before sampling period three years prior to the sale of the very *first* newspaper in that circulation group to be sold to a chain.

Using the same logic, Thrift made the after sampling period three years following the date of the *last* newspaper's purchase in that circulation group. This meant that three years was the *minimum* length of time for these newspapers to have settled into a routine under chain ownership.

In summary, the same sample of dates of publication was used within each circulation group, regardless of whether the newspaper was from the formerly independent group or from the comparison group of still-independent newspapers. These 18 dates, chosen randomly, came from at least three years before the formerly independent papers were purchased by a chain, with the "after" set of 18 dates from at least three years after purchase.

Defining Editorial "Vigor"

In effect, Thrift defined editorial "quality" as the proportion of newspaper editorials that displayed what he termed "vigor." Citing several discussions of what constituted vigor in newspaper editorials, Thrift said editorials had vigor when they

concerned local topics rather than issues located so far distant geographically that they were almost irrelevant to the immediate concerns of the audience;

argued for a viewpoint, rather than merely presenting information; and

concerned issues that were the subject of dispute and controversy.

Results of the Study

Thrift hoped to find that there were no differences in vigor between the editorials carried by the two groups of newspapers *prior to* purchase. The more similar the two groups' editorials were before the chain purchases, the easier it would be to point to chain ownership as the cause of whatever differences were found *after* the purchases.

As Thrift had hoped, the rates of vigorous editorials were almost identical for the two newspaper groups three or more years *before* the purchases, but differed substantially three or more years *after* chain ownership. Meanwhile, the proportion of vigorous editorials actually increased substantially for the still-independent comparison group, while it fell somewhat for the originally similar but now chain-owned papers. These patterns generally held across circulation groups.

The design of this study—with its before-after measures and its comparison group of matched independent newspapers—actually makes it a quasi-experiment. This design tremendously reduces the number of plausible rival explanations for the results. It is hard to see anything but purchase by a chain as the explanation for what happened to the relative vigor of these newspapers. Thus this empirical study provides strong support for social responsibility-style critics.

We now turn to a second study—and the choices its authors had to make. The study topic is not unrelated to the question of local vigor.

"AFGHANISTANISM" IN ENVIRONMENTAL NEWS

If vigor is reflected in editorials about local controversies, then its opposite is reflected in editorials about distant and far-removed places such as, say, Afghanistan. The term "Afghanistanism" came into use just after World War II, when a prominent editor criticized his colleagues for writing their most strongly worded editorials about controversies in places such as Afghanistan, located halfway around the world, while remaining silent about problems close to home. (Although the term is still used, it seems less appropriate now, since Afghanistan became a vital center of worldwide attention in the aftermath of the Soviet invasion and occupation of the country. It is no longer an "out of sight, out of mind" place.)

Afghanistanism needn't be true only of editorials. Many critics have speculated about similar patterns in the news, despite the greater news value traditionally attached to the "local angle." Earlier in this book, I presented examples of news stories that hometown media didn't cover, such as the "Sins of Sears" trial in Chicago and Warren Breed's (1958) analysis of stories that failed to appear in their communities' newspapers.

Afghanistanism especially might be a problem with environmental news because this news often concerns pollution allegedly caused by businesses and industry. Not only might those industries be important economic and political players in newspapers' communities, but local news media themselves have an economic interest in seeing their communities' businesses grow.

Hungerford and Lemert (1973) studied whether newspapers practiced Afghanistanism in their environmental news coverage. Their content analysis concerned all the daily newspapers then published in Oregon. Since Oregon has a national reputation for environmental consciousness, the underlying study rationale—an unspoken one, however—was that if Oregon's newspapers practiced environmental Afghanistanism, it would be hard to think of any other state's newspapers that would not.

Selecting Newspapers

Since there were fewer than two dozen daily newspapers in Oregon, it was easy for the researchers to decide to content-analyze every one of them.

Coding Locations

Given the importance of whether or not the story was located inside the newspaper's own circulation area, and given the distinct possibility that Oregon newspapers might carry more environmental news items about Oregon than newspapers in other, more typical states might carry about their own states, it seemed essential to the researchers to distinguish among locations of stories within the state. Oregon is composed of at least three remarkably distinct areas: (1) the fertile, relatively heavily populated Willamette Valley, (2) arid and sparsely populated Eastern Oregon, and (3) Southwest-Coastal Oregon, heavily dependent on tourism and natural resources, such as timber.

Hungerford and Lemert therefore decided to code story locations as follows:

- outside the state of Oregon
- in the Willamette Valley, outside the newspaper's circulation area
- in Eastern Oregon, outside the newspaper's circulation zone
- in Southwest and Coastal Oregon, outside the newspaper's circulation zone
- inside the newspaper's circulation zone

Since the Willamette Valley was the most industrialized, populous, and environmentally politicized geographic area of the state, it would be no surprise to discover that most of the Oregon-based stories might have Willamette Valley datelines (Salem, located in the Willamette Valley, is the state capital).

If it turned out, however, that most environmental stories were located in the Willamette Valley, why should we use the term *Afghanistanism* to describe such a result? After all, perhaps most other nonlocal stories also would have Willamette Valley datelines, since that's where the "action" would be.

A Variable for a Baseline

Anticipating an argument such as this led the researchers to create another variable (remember the "lust for variables"). The purpose of this new variable was to rebut the argument that findings for environmental news stories merely reflected where all the political action was in Oregon. The new variable was the subject of the news or editorial item, and it had two values: "environment" and "nonenvironment."

Provided with this new variable, the researchers were able to use the location of the *nonenvironmental* items as a baseline for assessing Afghanistanism in the environmental items. Are environmental stories as likely as the others to be located within the newspapers' own circulation areas? If not, where are the environmental stories displaced to?

Results

Hungerford and Lemert found that fewer than one in eight environmental stories was located in the newspapers' own cities, compared to more than one in four nonenvironmental stories. In addition, only one in sixteen environmental stories was located in the rest of each newspaper's own circulation area, compared to one in seven of the nonenvironmental stories. So environmental stories were more likely than other stories to be displaced away from the home territories of Oregon's daily newspapers. Tellingly, environmental stories were *more* likely than the other stories to be written *by local staff*, but less likely than other stories to be *about* local issues.

Where were the environmental stories displaced to? Not outside Oregon—35% of the environmental stories were located out of state, compared to 42% of the other stories. Instead, they were displaced to "up the road a piece"—someplace else in Oregon. For newspapers located in the Willamette Valley, environmental stories were more likely than other stories to be located somewhere else in the Valley. For Eastern Oregon and Southwest-Coastal Oregon newspapers, Oregon environmental items were also far more likely than other stories to be located in the Willamette Valley.

Since we've used the other stories as a baseline, it can't be said that the "tilt" of environmental stories toward the Willamette Valley is the normal and expected result of concentrating Oregon's population, industry, and political centers in the Valley. If it were such a "normal" result, we would expect to find *nonenvironmental* news stories to be located there as commonly as were the environmental stories. That didn't happen.

Even when environmental news stories were located within a newspaper's own region, environmental coverage was not often about situations within that newspaper's own city or circulation area, while the other news stories almost always were. Clearly, the displacement away of environmental stories was *not* due to the fact that local reporters weren't covering them. They were, substantially more often than they covered stories about other topics. In other words, these findings have no easy explanation other than environmental Afghanistanism.

While this study's design wasn't nearly as complex as Thrift's chain-ownership study, Afghanistanism research did need to create that baseline of nonenvironmental news to eliminate the most plausible rival explanations for the results. Once again, our lust for variables created that baseline for us.

Our next study example also was a content analysis, demonstrating a different way of solving the problem of providing a baseline for comparisons.

A CRITIQUE OF RAPE COVERAGE

Like murder and assault, rape is a crime committed by one human being against another. Unlike these crimes, however, rape poses a special problem for journalists—they feel very uncomfortable about reporting the names of rape victims (probably for what are good reasons in our culture), so they generally withhold victims' names.

Some feminists feel that withholding the names of rape victims from the news unintentionally communicates to audiences that rapes are somehow the "fault" of the victim, since victims of other violent crimes often are named. Perhaps this selective naming of victims does communicate that message, but rape victims already are likely to be "put on trial" and forced to defend and explain their dress, actions, and even past lives if and when a rape case goes to trial. Certainly, about the last thing a rape victim wants to see is her name in the paper, according to interviews with journalists reporting on those crimes. A survey of newspaper decision makers by journalism professor Carol Oukrop (1983) confirmed that these journalists are strongly opposed to reporting rape victims' names. Clearly, what the journalists are trying to do is to protect rape victims' right to privacy.

While Schwengels and Lemert (1986) agreed with the need to prevent any further invasion of the rape victim's privacy, it seemed to them that the ways journalists protect victims' privacy might seriously mislead *future* rape victims about where—and against whom—they should take protective measures. In other words, in journalists' efforts to protect the privacy of victims, might they not be failing to give potential victims "fair warning"? Schwengels and Lemert suspected, for example, that the threat of incestuous rapes would almost be ignored in the news, since it would be hard to identify the accused rapist without so greatly narrowing down the list of possible victims that it would be easy to figure out the actual victim's name. They suspected, as well, that, since most incestuous rapes are committed in homes and other surroundings familiar to the victim, newspaper content would communicate the misleading impression that typical rapists are shadowy strangers who lurk only in the "dangerous" parts of town.

The only previous content-analytic study to focus primarily on rape news reported finding two major differences between newspaper coverage of rape and coverage of other crimes against people (Heath et al., 1981):

- Metropolitan dailies underreported rape crimes in comparison to their presence in the Uniform Crime Statistics (UCS) for cities included in the study.
- Stories about rape withheld many more details about the crime, including— but not limited to—the identities of victims.

Problems with the UCS Baseline

While Schwengels and Lemert had little reason to dispute these findings, they felt the findings were more vulnerable to other explanations than they needed to be. First, there might be a longer time lag between the crime of rape and the reporting of it to police than for other crimes. Rape victims might be considerably more ambivalent than other victims about reporting the crime, so that they more often delay reporting it. In contrast with other crimes, then, the Uniform Crime Statistics for a given year might not be fully comparable to rape news reports for that "same" year. More specifically, the UCS might be back-dated with, say, late-December rapes included in the statistics, when the rapes themselves might not have been reported to police until the following year. Obviously, no journalist could report the story until the crime had been reported to the police. Comparing news reports of rapes against the UCS might thus build into that comparison whatever discrepancies there might be between the period covered by the statistics and the publication cycle of newspapers.

A second possible problem with merely comparing crime news content against statistics generated from law enforcement records is that the researchers couldn't be sure how complete the police reports actually were at the time they were shown to reporters. Given that they weren't using the original police reports, they had no way of knowing whether stories about rapes left out some details because police—not journalists—were less willing to provide those details when the crime was rape.

A Better Baseline

The answer to these problems was to compare news stories about rapes with the police reports concerning those rapes. Any discrepancies between the two would result from the decisions of journalists—not police—to withhold information.

With some difficulty, the researchers managed to convince law enforcement authorities of Lane County, Oregon, to allow access to the written police reports about the crimes. They compared the police reports about rape filed in all jurisdictions for the year against all the stories about rape carried by the county's only daily, the *Register-Guard*.

Results

More than half the year's 89 rape cases were committed by persons well known to the victims, yet 60% of all the news stories concerned rapes by strangers. Only 35 of the 89 cases were covered at all, with stories about the year's 21 incestuous rapes (reported to the police) almost completely missing from the news.

While 3 of the 21 incestuous rapes did receive news coverage, they were not reported as incestuous rapes; instead, news stories made them look like "stranger" rapes. Why? Because, in each case, the story was based on the arrest of the suspect. To have mentioned that the alleged crime was incestuous would have virtually identified the victim. Interestingly, another eight men were arrested on grounds of incestuous rape, but those eight arrests received no coverage at all. Neither did the ten reported cases of incestuous rape in which no arrest had yet been made.

Schwengels and Lemert found other important discrepancies between police and news reports. Some of these discrepancies involved information that might have helped women make better judgments about whether to use force in attempting to defend themselves against attackers. While more than half the police reports described whether or not—and how—the victim tried to defend herself, hardly any of the news stories did. Similarly, while all the police reports covered the assailant's use or nonuse of force, more than a third of the news stories did not. While police reports almost always contained information about injuries to the victim, news reports hardly ever did. In contrast to police reports, news stories also rarely mentioned whether or not the victim received medical treatment.

In almost 70% of the rape stories, the victim's first contact with her assailant was outside the home, while the actual location of more than half of all the first contacts was in the home. Therefore, if women used the news to decide where they would be in the most danger, they would decide that the greatest peril lay in the outside world.

The news can provide "fair warning" to women in another way, however—by realistically describing the rapists themselves. What happened to this sort of information in the police reports? Although almost all police reports gave the assailant's apparent age, almost a third of the news stories did not. The news was especially likely not to report age when the assailant was 35 or older. The marital status of the assailant was never given in news stories, even though 35% of the police reports provided that information. (When the victim's marital status was given, both in police and news reports, it was "single" almost every time.)

Some of the misleading portrayal of rape clearly resulted from the newspaper's avoidance of incestuous rape stories. Even in the three cases in which arrests for incestuous rapes were reported, the news account made the alleged crime appear to have been a routine "stranger" rape—mostly that appearance was created by what was not said, rather than what was—by reporting the ages of victims of incest in the same way that ages of "routine" victims were reported, and by not mentioning the circumstances of the rape.

Suggestions for Improvement

Schwengels and Lemert's (1986) original research article offers a "model" story for incestuous rape coverage that demonstrates methods of preventing disclosure of the victim's identity while making it possible to alert readers routinely to the prevalence of incestuous rape and similar rapes perpetrated by "friends of the family." The model story achieves these ends by deleting the names of both rapist and victim, while explicitly pointing out that the alleged crime was incestuous rape.

The actual published reports differed from the "reality" of the police reports, however, in many ways. Only part of these discrepancies resulted from newspaper avoidance of incestuous rape coverage. Discrepancies continued even after these cases were deleted. These discrepancies raise important questions about how misleading the portrayal of rape victimization can be to women who rely on news reports. Judging from this sample of news stories, women

who are single are at the most risk;

should fear strangers more than men who are known to them;

should fear men younger than 35 years of age;
apparently didn't try to defend themselves against rapists;
didn't need medical attention and weren't injured in any significant way; and
were at greatest risk when they ventured from home.

Women who relied on their newspapers to help them make decisions about where and with whom rape was a high risk would be misled in important ways about the risks they actually would face. In the case of rape, what women don't know can hurt them.

If the purpose of criticism is to promote constructive change, such research as the foregoing content analysis—and the model story derived from it—is offered in that spirit. The research design—by directly comparing the information on the police report forms with what the newspaper reported—virtually eliminates the possibility that "fair warning" wasn't given female readers because journalists didn't have the information available in the first place.

A similar task—to eliminate a plausible rival explanation that would have shifted the "blame" elsewhere—was at the center of the next critical study.

"WHODUNIT?"

Earlier, we saw that mobilizing information is often missing from news stories concerning political controversies, but is often provided in news stories with a "positive" context (e.g., a story about a pharmacy offering low-cost prescription drugs to the elderly). However, before we can be certain that it was *journalists* who blocked this information from news about politics, we need to eliminate another possibility—and see what occurs. The other possibility is that journalists don't usually have the MI to report when they write stories about political controversies. Perhaps politicians "dry up" when they are embroiled in controversy, withholding any relevant mobilizing information from journalists. If this were occurring, we'd still see the same pattern in the content analysis—MI in positive contexts and almost no MI in controversial ones—but the rival explanation would be that it was news sources, not journalists, who withheld the MI.

Two Ways to See "Whodunit"

In broad terms, we have available to us two methods for discovering whether it is the sources—not the journalists—who withhold the MI from controversial stories. The first method would be to select, in some fashion, a large and diverse array of potential news stories—some with positive context and some controversial—and follow them from the story idea through information gathering, writing, editing, and, finally, to broadcast or print publication. To do the study in this fashion *could* produce "naturalistic" results with numerous obvious applications to journalism. Unfortunately, this study would be extremely time-consuming and costly, and would ultimately be vulnerable to questions about how representative of the samples of sources, journalists, and stories were. Ideally, one might even want to observe what the *same* source provided to journalists in *each* context: controversial and positive. To capture such an ideal, balanced comparison for each source might require an extremely long wait.

The second broad approach would be a controlled experiment in which the same MI is given to journalists, but the context of the story is manipulated. If journalists then cut out more of the MI when the story context is controversial, this discrepancy obviously could not be the result of sources withholding MI from journalists. As journalists would have the MI in both cases, the discrepancy would have to result from the journalists' reaction to context. This was the reasoning I used in an experiment performed with the cooperation of 56 experienced newspaper, wire service, and bureau journalists (Lemert, 1984).

The Experiment

The professional journalists all were interviewed and tested at their job sites. Told that a study of "editing" was being conducted, the journalists were handed two typewritten stories to edit. The first story was used for "warm-up" purposes; the second was the experimental story.

What the journalists didn't know was that half of them received one version of the experimental story and the others—often sitting near them—received the other. The MI in both versions was identical ("method of constancy"). The locations in the stories of the three separate bits of MI were identical as well. Both versions of the story were the same number of paragraphs in length and were typeset to appear identical in number of lines. The principal subject of both versions also was the same—beetles were devastating forests in the Pacific Northwest. By changing a few words, however, one version of the story was made into a story about a controversy, and the other version was left as a positive-context story. The two versions of the story can be illustrated by contrasting the two lead paragraphs:

Positive-context lead: Another wave of bugs may be destroying huge amounts of Douglas fir.

Controversial-context lead: Another wave of bugs may be destroying huge amounts of Douglas fir—and stimulating pressure for use again of the controversial pesticide DDT to control it.

While attacks on trees by a pest are not exactly "positive" news to anyone, the positive-context story nevertheless contained no hint of controversy and could easily have been the sort of story that would run on a newspaper's gardening page or even in its business section. Since everyone would agree that the bugs should be stopped, this was not a controversial story. In contrast, the mention of DDT immediately politicized the other version of the story.

As mentioned, each journalist read and edited only one of the two versions. After the 56 journalists had turned in their edited stories, they completed a brief questionnaire concerning their reactions to the story.

Results

When the MI was in the controversial-context version, the journalists cut it out much more frequently than when it appeared in the positive-context version. Furthermore, when asked to choose entire paragraphs to be eliminated if their story had to be cut some more, the journalists in the controversial-context group cut paragraphs *with MI* in them far more often than did the other journalists.

Clearly, then, journalists seem to be responsible for at least part of the near disappearance of MI from stories about issues that would arouse a desire to express one's views about a matter of public controversy. The power of lobbyists and "insiders" to influence political outcomes is thus maintained—even enhanced—when ordinary citizens are cut off from relevant MI every time there is a political controversy.

The behavior of journalists when confronted with MI would tend to reduce the numbers of citizens who are able to influence legislation and other political-bureaucratic decisions. On the face of it, this behavior seems to be inconsistent with the rhetoric of journalism. Journalists assert that they "do" journalism to inform the citizenry and to enhance popular participation in public affairs. As the foregoing study has illustrated, however, the "fit" between journalists' professed intentions and their performance can be poor at times.

As the last set of illustrative studies, we turn now to several different ways of testing the "official source" bias in the news.

THE OFFICIAL SOURCE SYNDROME

One of the most common complaints to be made about journalism in America is its dependence on "official sources" (see Chapters 1 and 2 for earlier treatments of this topic). In brief, journalists have, in effect, reduced the question of "objectivity"—so goes my earlier argument—to the question of whether the most obvious and defensible sources are used. As long as the sources who would immediately occur to reporters' editors have been sought and used in "touchy" stories, "objectivity" has been adhered to.

The most obvious and defensible sources are "official" sources—those located on the reporters' beats, which, themselves, tend to be organized around "official" agencies (police, fire, city government). "Official" sources from these "official" agencies tend to have "official" titles, too. It would be unusual if reporters were to interview secretaries of these officials—it would perhaps result in a better story, but certainly an unusual one.

We saw in Chapter 4 how the official source syndrome has been tested through an experiment in which two persons testifying to a city council said equally newsworthy things (Schwantes and Lemert, 1978). Even though his statements to the council literally were interchangeable with the statements made by the unaffiliated source, the neighborhood group representative was preferred as the news source by the Reporting I student writers. This study was an experiment, combined with content analysis of the students' stories.

Covering the Statehouse

In other research, journalism professors Tony Atwater and Fred Fico (1986) combined a survey with content analysis in a unique setting—the Statehouse, where the Michigan State Legislature meets. The researchers were interested in whether print and broadcast journalists depend equally on news events staged for them by "official" sources. Reasoning that most general-assignment broadcast reporters are handicapped because they must chase from scene to scene after many different stories, Atwater and Fico chose to study a beat where both print and broadcast reporters could stay with the same stories all day—if they wanted to. Since they were studying reporters assigned to cover the Michigan Statehouse, Atwater and Fico, in effect, held preparation time and background information constant. Thus any differences between print and broadcast reports presumably could not be laid to differences in time and background information. The trade-off in limiting their study to the Statehouse, of course, was to raise questions about whether their findings could be generalized to any other groups of reporters or other beats.

That Baseline Again

Since Atwater and Fico were comparing news reports across media, print-media reporters provided that much-desired baseline against which broadcast reports could be measured—and vice versa.

Results

What did the two researchers find? While many of the sources used were similar, broadcast reporters relied much more heavily than newspaper reporters on material from prearranged, staged, and predictable events such as news conferences. Newspaper reporters said that they relied on printed documents for their stories much more often than broadcast reporters did. Atwater and Fico concluded that newspaper stories displayed more evidence of initiative than did broadcast stories and also conveyed a wider array of perspectives than was available via broadcast news. Broadcast news tended to "load up" on officials who were already visible and widely known, presumably because broadcast journalists were more likely than print ones to think their audiences needed to be provided information through such obviously well-known and familiar sources.

This study used two methods: a survey of reporters and content analysis of their reports. Of course, their results may be specific to Statehouse reporting. However, we've already seen one of the things that can happen when multiple researchers attack the same problem, using different methods and studying different situations: Similar results from different methods, obtained from distinctly different news agencies, lend confidence and generalizability to both the original findings—and the criticisms—of media behavior.

A "Pure" Content Analysis

Let me add one more study to the mix of "official source" findings, pointing out again some of the choices and trade-offs researchers make. Researcher Jane Brown and her colleagues (1982) emphatically pointed out that content analysis as a method captures only the end product of pressures and other forces that the content itself may not adequately reveal. Nevertheless, they decided to limit their study to content analysis, presumably justifying their choice in a couple of ways:

- The last major content-analytic demonstration of the official source bias had occurred 10 years before. It needed to be updated and could be used, as well, to see if changes in the news industry had produced changes in official source news habits.
- The researchers provided three reasonably well-developed competing explanations that provided rival value systems with which the content analysis results themselves could be evaluated. (While these rival explanations hint at different forces that could have produced the same news content, Brown et al. concede that there is no way one can choose among the three rival explanations based on the results themselves. This certainly is the weak point of their decision to analyze only the content.)

One Baseline. On the one hand, by choosing to study newspaper content only, the researchers sacrificed the chance to compare broadcast to print media. On the other hand, they did build into their study another kind of baseline comparison. They sampled the front-page stories in the *New York Times* and *Washington Post*, treating them as their "national" newspapers, and sampled as well four North Carolina newspapers, treating these as their "local" newspaper group. In addition, they created a third value of their variable by separating from both newspaper groups all the front-page wire service stories and treating these as a third group of stories. Thus whatever the "national" papers did could be compared against each of the other local and "wire" groups, and vice versa.

A Second Baseline. In addition, the researchers deliberately chose to sample the two national newspapers in such a way as to allow direct comparability with results obtained for the same papers 10 years earlier, so the time variable provided another baseline, if necessary.

A Control for Story Location. Since all the stories appeared on the front pages (breakovers of the same stories to back pages were included), the location in the paper was held constant. Thus differences among the three groups of news agencies couldn't be due to the location of the stories.

Randomization. Finally, since the three samples of stories were chosen by chance, randomization was used as a last defense to pretty much wipe out the influence of other, otherwise-uncontrolled variables.

Results. On balance, the researchers found that the similarities among the three groups of news agencies outweighed the differences. They found, for example, that government officials as sources dominated front-page news, regardless of whether the story were done by the wire services, the local newspapers, or the two national ones. Unfortunately, when you get a result like this—when you find all of your news agencies have behaved similarly—you may be without any basis for saying whether whatever you found is "too much"—or "too little." Fortunately for Brown et al., many other researchers have provided baselines against which the dependence on official sources can be judged as too high (see, for example, Roshco, 1975: chap. 6).

In addition, Brown et al. found that the next most common source—individuals who were affiliated with groups—outnumbered unaffiliated individual sources by almost six to one (this finding is quite consistent with the experiment by Schwantes and Lemert, 1978). When sources were broken down by their status within their government or private organizations, all three news agency groups showed an overwhelming "tilt" toward printing statements by people from the top of the organizational hierarchy, rather than from the bottom. In most cases, the next most common source position was as a "spokesperson" for the organization. Persons coded as "workers" (secretaries and the like) overall were least likely to be used as sources, although there were some differences among the media groups here. Local newspapers were more likely to use "workers" than "spokespersons" as sources in their stories about state and local government, though use of both groups as sources still fell far below use of top executives.

Local newspapers seemed much more likely than the wire services and national newspapers to cover stories that required personal initiative and enterprise. In contrast, both the more prestigious *New York Times* and *Washington Post* seemed predisposed to cover the routine, prearranged press conference and staged event. Famed for investigative initiative in the early days of Watergate, the *Post*'s front pages bore more resemblance to the kind of convenient stories used by Michigan Statehouse television reporters than to the more evenly balanced pages of four smallish North Carolina dailies. Because the researchers found a difference here among the news agency groups—an embarrassing one, if one works for either of the two prestige newspapers—the higher "initiative" rate for the smaller papers acts as a baseline against which the lower rate for the others looks too low. This may cause someone to ask, "If smaller papers can show that much initiative, why can't the two papers with greater resources and important reputations?"

SUMMARY AND OVERVIEW

This chapter has considered empirical research in five areas of criticism:

- what happens to editorial vigor in newspapers after they've been acquired by a chain;
- Afghanistanism in environmental news;
- how the best of intentions in rape coverage can leave women without "fair warning" concerning the nature, location, and character of the threat of rape to them and their children;
- whether or not journalists selectively cut out mobilizing information when it is given to them; and
- different ways to document the official source bias in journalism.

In each of these areas, I have tried to encourage readers to imagine themselves in the role of the researcher, having to make the hard choices that needed to be made before the data could be gathered. Often these decisions involved how to create baselines for comparison (e.g., the "original" police reports, nonenvironmental news items, the vigor of editorials in still-independent newspapers). It is these comparative baselines that allow us to argue that the rate of something happening (e.g., vigor in chain newspapers, or local environmental news) is too low, and therefore should be criticized.

The research we examined used many of the tools in the empirical tool bag: the experiment, content analysis, the survey, and the quasi-experiment.

Space does not permit presentation of how random sampling is done or how to calculate a statistical significance test. However, several useful books already have covered these points. A basic introduction for those wanting to learn about statistical tests is the aptly titled *No-Frills Statistics*, by Susan Gray (1983). Although it is an older book, Fred Kerlinger's *Foundations of Behavioral Research* (1973) provides an excellent introduction to variables and hypotheses, along with more advanced chapters on research design and sampling.

REFERENCES

ATWATER, T. and F. FICO (1986) "Source reliance and use in reporting state government: a study of print and broadcast practices." Newspaper Research Journal 8 (Fall): 53-61.
BREED, W. (1958) "Mass communication and sociocultural integration." Social Forces 37 (December): 109-116.

BROWN, J. D., C. R. BYBEE, S. T. WEARDEN, and D. MURDOCK (1982) "Invisible power: news sources and the limits of diversity." Presented at the annual meeting of the Association for Education in Journalism and Mass Communication, Ohio University, July.

GRAY, S. H. (1983) No-Frills Statistics: A Guide for the First-Year Student. Totowa, NJ: Rowman & Allanheld.

HEATH, L., M. T. GORDON, and R. LEBAILLY (1981) "What newspapers tell us (and don't tell us) about rape." Newspaper Research Journal 2 (July): 48-55.

HUNGERFORD, S. E. and J. B. LEMERT (1973) "Covering the environment: a new 'Afghanistanism'?" Journalism Quarterly 50 (Autumn): 475-481, 508.

KERLINGER, F. N. (1973) Foundations of Behavioral Research (2nd ed.). New York: Holt, Rinehart & Winston.

LEMERT, J. B. (1984) "Name context and the elimination of mobilizing information: an experiment." Journalism Quarterly 61 (Summer): 243-249, 259.

OAKES, J. B. (1968) "The editorial page." Nieman Reports 22 (September): 2, 8.

OUKROP, C. E. (1983) "Views of newspaper gatekeepers on rape and rape coverage." Presented at the annual meeting of the Association for Education in Journalism and Mass Communication, Oregon State University, August.

ROSHCO, B. (1975) Newsmaking. Chicago: University of Chicago Press.

SCHWANTES, D. L. and J. B. LEMERT (1978) "Media access as a function of source-group identity." Journalism Quarterly 55 (Winter): 772-775.

SCHWENGELS, M. and J. B. LEMERT (1986) "Fair warning: a comparison of police and newspaper reports of rape." Newspaper Research Journal 7 (Spring): 35-42.

THRIFT, R. R., Jr. (1977) "How chain ownership affects editorial vigor of newspapers." Journalism Quarterly 54 (Summer): 327-331.

7

SYSTEMATIC CRITICISM AND MEDIA STUDIES

Three popular, but false, truisms about empirical criticism are presented, along with some ideas for critical studies.

A thoughtful, systematic analysis of news conventions offers plenty of room for all of the scholarly approaches discussed in this book—empirical, Marxist, social responsibility, and cultural/critical studies, as well as those "fuzzy" variants representing combinations of these four. Empirical study of news performance, however, is the one approach that is most often overlooked.

THREE FALSE TRUISMS

Three false, yet popular, ideas have plagued empirically based criticism which relies on social science methods:

- *Empirical research is essentially "administrative" in character.* This is just not so. This book has highlighted many studies aimed at current media pretenses and practices. Ralph Thrift (1977), for instance, showed that the vigor of a newspaper's editorials falls when it is taken over by a chain. My own research on MI confronts journalists with their own rhetoric about their obligation to provide the public with the information it needs.

- *Empirical research worries about making the media more efficient and is therefore not critical.* Even when "administrative" empirical researchers could be said to have in mind "efficiency" in achieving the media organization's goals, it still doesn't follow that this research isn't tough-minded and sometimes quite critical of media and media practices. Mark Levy and John Robinson (1986) found, for instance, that network television news currently is quite inept at organizing stories that their audiences can easily understand. Among changes that Levy and Robinson suggest is that network news should cut distracting visuals that interfere with their stories' verbal content.

• *Media effects studies always support the status quo and the media's profit-making goals.* It also is not true that all studies testing media effects automatically take on a slavish, pandering character. As soon as one looks for effects that don't fit into the commercially defined goals of media management, the way lies open for considering whether those "other" effects are socially desirable. Does the crime rate go down when there aren't any newspapers? Do the news media widen the knowledge gap among citizens when they publicize a given news topic? Do the news media eliminate numerous presidential candidates from primaries long before most voters have any information at all about those candidates? These are "effects" questions, as are many others posed by studies cited in this book. If such effects are demonstrated, *there is a consensus in our culture about the evaluation to be attached to each effect.* Nobody except the criminal approves of crime. The media are supposed to shrink knowledge gaps, not widen them! How can we be sure we have the best candidates if many of them are eliminated before voters even learn their names? In each case, the evaluation attached to the effect is obvious. In short, empirical researchers try to do impartial work. They should neither be cheerleaders for the media nor harsh, uncaring critics.

CRITERIA FOR A CRITICAL TRADITION

Social responsibility theory embodies these consensual values and, in that sense, comes as close as any critical approach to fulfilling one major requirement that Brown (1974: 17-20) deems necessary for any sustained tradition of media criticism: a set of shared, preestablished values that can be used to evaluate media performance. Despite the industry's initial resistance to the 1947 report of the Commission on the Freedom of the Press, the ideas embodied in social responsibility theory are now widely shared among U.S. journalists, many critics, and the public at large.

It was no accident that Chapter 5 drew connections between empirical research results and social responsibility-based concerns about media performance. While social responsibility theory comes as close as any of our four schools of criticism to embodying values shared by journalists, critics, and the public, social responsibility theory itself is mute concerning the methods one would use to create evidence of media performance. Historically, social responsibility assumptions commonly underlie almost all the case studies and anecdotes reported in the journalism reviews. I hope that Chapter 5 made it obvious, however, that social responsibility values are perfectly compatible with the gathering of data through systematic empirical research. Because of the baselines that are almost automatically provided through the "lust for variables," my own prejudices favor using empirical research methods on all problems on which it is appropriate to use those methodologies. In other words, where the anecdotal method and the empirical method each can be applied appropriately, *the latter usually will produce more defensible evidence.*

Although both anecdotal and empirical social science methods can be communicated to and understood by others, the former probably is *easier* to understand. The critic who generalizes from examples, however, is always vulnerable to accusations of selecting only the examples that "fit." Furthermore, when the evidence is anecdotal, there always is the troubling problem of the lack of a baseline for comparison. Therefore, my argument is that, on balance, empirical social science comes closer to fulfilling a second criterion for a successful critical tradition: It uses methods that can be communicated to others who are then able to retest those findings, if they so wish.

Remember that we are still considering topics that can be examined equally well anecdotally or through empirical social science techniques. I'm not arguing that empirical techniques are as applicable to every topic as some other techniques might be. Marxist, cultural/critical studies, and social responsibility critics have raised some questions about media performance that have not yet been addressed effectively through empirical social science techniques.

SOME IDEAS FOR STUDIES

What, then, are the sorts of questions that can appropriately be studied through empirical communication research? Following are some examples, and I invite you to add to them. Remember the criteria for good research hypotheses (see Chapter 4).

(1) In a thoughtful column about the press and the sex scandal that ended Gary Hart's bid for the presidency, David S. Broder (1987) concluded: "The indictment of American journalism is not that we go too far [in examining the record, past policy views, and character of presidential candidates], but that we too often don't dig deep enough and say plainly what we have found." We saw in Chapter 5 that the news media seem institutionally unable or unwilling to give equal coverage to all presidential contenders, to provide voters with much information about candidates' current policy proposals, and candidates' character and qualifications. What about candidates' past records? Is Broder right about that, too?

Obviously, one could use a home VCR to record (say) one network's coverage of candidates' past records versus their present policy views, as well as other types of coverage of candidates (e.g., the "horse race" aspects). We already suspect strongly that scant network time will be spent covering candidates' *present* policy views—would even fewer minutes be given to candidates' past records? If two of the candidates are governors, how much time do you suppose would be given to comparing their administrative "styles"? If two candidates are legislators, how much time do you suppose would be given to coverage of their past legislative records, their ability to work with colleagues, their proportion of missed roll-call votes, and so on? Do media-declared "front-runners" get more coverage of their past records, or more coverage of how in the past they *became* front-runners?

Given the precedent of the Hart scandal, when and under what conditions are journalists likely to ask about candidates' sex histories? Given the insidious spread of the AIDS epidemic, are journalists more likely now than they were in the past to ask candidates about their "morality"?

In any case, a comparative historical baseline for such a study of TV news can be established by using the network news archives at Vanderbilt University. In the case of newspapers, your university library probably has the resources to allow you to search past issues and establish a print news baseline.

(2) Despite the media's vigorous minority recruiting efforts, few black Americans seem attracted to news reporting, especially when that reporting would be for newspapers. If literacy levels of blacks and whites are held constant, are blacks less attracted than whites to newspapers because middle-class, white newspaper people are unintentionally sending black readers a latent message not being sent in broadcast news? (This could be described as administrative research with highly critical implications!) If so, is this latent print message being received only by blacks, and not by equally literate whites? Interviews with blacks could be used to determine what they understand the message to be.

(3) We saw earlier that race is less often mentioned in crime news. If race is mentioned, however, it tends to be that of a racial minority. Being white, in other words, is taken for granted. As the proportion of minority members increases in a community, though, is a person's race more likely—or less likely—to be explicitly mentioned in the news? The most straightforward way to perform this study would be to compare news media in different sections of the country today. Do broadcast

news reporters verbally refer to race less often than newspaper people do? If so, do the electronic newscasters substitute pictures or other indicators of race more often than newspapers do? Remember the study of sportscasters and the race of pro football players.

(4) Are negative- or controversial-context stories about local businesses more likely to be originated by wire services or other nonlocal news services than positive-context stories about local businesses? Such a study can be done using a fairly straightforward content analysis, though the sample of newspapers might have to be large enough to allow for collection of 30 or 40 negative/controversial stories about local business.

(5) "Tactical" mobilizing information is MI that provides behavioral guidance. That guidance can be explicit, for instance, illustrated by stories that encourage the listener or reader to try a recipe or follow some gardening tips. It can also be more implicit, illustrated by crime stories that describe in some detail how a gas station was held up at night or how a methamphetamine lab was concealed. Presumably, in providing crime modus operandi, the reporter isn't advocating that the audience try the same exploit, so perhaps the reporter feels no responsibility for providing the criminal MI. (Another rationale for providing the modus operandi in crime news may be that it warns potential victims. Journalists who employ this justification don't bother to confront the problem that there are thousands more victims—each of whom presumably would have to be forewarned by the MI—while all it takes is one "copycat" criminal to have been informed of the modus operandi.)

Are journalists more likely to report tactical MI when it would appear in a crime news story than in news about politics? If so, why are there lower barriers to tactical MI in crime stories than in political stories? One way to carry out this study would be to write a crime story and a political story, each containing a similar type of tactical MI, and then show the stories to journalists, asking them to edit the two stories.

(6) Sometimes one of the best ways to convince media personnel to make changes suggested by critical research is to show how those changes will help them enlarge their audience or beef up profits. Since "efficiency" is the operating goal of administrative research, if you can provide convincing evidence that media can more efficiently hang onto and attract audiences, you can disguise a fundamentally critical recommendation in the clothing of an administrative research study.

In an unpublished study, Lemert and Murphy (1988) used a market-research-style "intercept" survey of 521 shoppers to test whether readers preferred news stories with MI in them over otherwise-identical stories that lacked only the MI. Some 260 of the shoppers were shown the MI and no-MI versions of a story about politics and the other 261 were shown the two versions of a story about a consumer matter. In order to avoid bias, neither the MI in the stories nor the concept of MI was ever referred to, let alone explained to respondents. However, if respondents actually read both of the nearly identical stories, the MI difference was readily apparent. Since respondents saw the two versions, side-by-side on the same page, most were able to detect the MI difference.

The political story concerned a controversial bill supposedly pending at the Oregon legislature. The bill would change whether corporations could be held financially responsible for "accidental" discharges of pollutants. One legislator favoring the bill and another opposing it were quoted in the article. The version with MI provided the office addresses and phone numbers of the two legislators, plus a toll-free number that would connect with the Capitol switchboard.

The consumer story concerned a warning by a state official that firewood buyers should beware of claims by dealers about how much wood was being delivered. The version with MI gave the office phone number of the official and stated that any claim that a pickup load constituted a cord of wood almost certainly was false. The version lacking the MI did not provide the phone number and merely said that pickup loads "varied considerably."

As Table 7.1 shows, most of the shoppers said they would prefer to see the MI version in their newspaper. The majorities preferring the MI version got even bigger when we looked only at those who actually noticed the presence of MI in one version and the absence in the other.

Tellingly, very few of the large numbers of people who noticed the MI thought their newspaper would choose to run that MI version. However, these respondents were *relatively* more likely to think their paper's editors would run the MI version in the consumer context.

Table 7.2 presents the results concerning respondents' perceptions of newspaper willingness to carry the version with MI.

One of the more interesting conclusions suggested by these results was that, despite the fact that MI was neither explained nor even pointed out to these respondents, they were rather accurate in their perceptions of the relative odds against MI for each topic. Many of our content studies show that the odds against MI go way up when we move from relatively "positive" contexts like firewood supplies to a controversial political battle over a legislative proposal.

TABLE 7.1

| Story Topic | Percentages Choosing MI Version of Story: | |
	Among All Respondents	Among Those Who Noticed MI
Politics	53.8% (N = 260)	61.6% (N = 216)
Consumer	73.9% (N = 261)	80.6% (N = 232)

All of this leads me to suggest a new study. If audiences have accurate perceptions of news media behavior regarding MI, how accurate would journalists be in estimating audience interest in MI? Would the journalists be more likely to underestimate audience interest in the political MI than in the consumer MI?

To investigate the accuracy of journalists' perceptions of audience interest, one would need to interview both journalists and audience members, showing them the MI and non-MI versions of each story, and asking the journalists to estimate percentages of audience choices.

(7) In some communities, "alternative" newspapers explicitly consider themselves to be providing a genuine alternative to the mainstream community newspaper(s). Is the quality of local news coverage improved in the mainstream daily when it is challenged by such an alternative paper? In other words, does the public have a stake in preserving and supporting such "alternative" papers—not so much because of what these papers do, but because of what they challenge the mainstream daily to do? To perform this study, one would have to try to match cities on as many other characteristics as possible, then do a content analysis of their mainstream dailies' local news content. The independent variable would be the existence or nonexistence of a feisty "alternative" paper in town.

(8) To follow up the Afghanistanism study, one could investigate whether environmental stories by local staffers—but located outside the newspaper's circulation zone or the station's primary market—are more likely to involve a controversy about business or industry than when the locally staffed environmental story is datelined inside the circulation zone or primary market. In other words, when environmental Afghanistanism occurs, is it because the controversy concerns business? We can also ask a slightly different question: When local staffers do an environmental story, will it be located more often outside the primary market when it involves a controversy than when it doesn't? Such a study would employ a fairly straightforward content analysis, but one

TABLE 7.2

Percentage of People Who Noticed MI But Said Their Newspaper Would Not Carry the Story with MI

Story Topic	My Newspaper Would Run:	
	Version Lacking MI	*Version With MI*
Political (N = 216)	90.3%	9.7%
Consumer (N = 232)	67.2%	32.8%

would have to be able to identify whether the environmental story was done by local staff.

(9) A final example of a critical empirical study flows from the often-heard social responsibility complaint that the news media ignore the flaws and failings of their competitors—perhaps in fear that, otherwise, their competitors might take revenge and eventually do the same to them. One method for studying how news media organizations cover their competitors would be to use a newspaper/broadcasting industry magazine—such as *Editor & Publisher* or *Broadcasting*—to locate controversies concerning the business aspects of a particular newspaper or station. The controversy might, for instance, concern rumors of owners' wish to sell, a challenge to broadcast license renewal, or clashes between news staff and management.

To conduct such a study, one could compare coverage (or lack of it) in the target news agency against coverage by one or more of the following baseline groups: (1) its rivals within the same market, (2) media nearby but not in the same market and not under the same ownership, (3) "national" media that tell the public about news industry problems (the *Los Angeles Times* and *Washington Post* are obvious examples), and (4) across media (e.g., in radio when the controversy concerns TV or newspapers; in magazines when the controversy concerns newspapers or TV). A number of such business-related cases probably can be assembled, and content analyses done.

That's just a sample of possibilities. Of course, almost any one of the studies mentioned previously in this book offers a prime chance to see if its results would apply to the media in your own area.

You don't have to be a statistical wizard to do these studies, either. If you can calculate percentages, that probably will be sufficient mathematical treatment for most purposes. Remember that most journalists who will need to be persuaded to make changes aren't statistical wizards, either.

CONCLUSION

Few Western institutions are as often noticed—and as often resented—as the news media. Given their affluence, importance, and visibility in modern Western societies, the news media themselves should long ago have fostered a tradition of informed and sustained self-examination. Given news media reluctance to commission such self-examination, what may be even more surprising is that nobody else has noticeably succeeded in establishing such a tradition, either.

It is time for divided and bickering critics to emphasize the things we have in common—a wish to examine news media traditions, omissions, and commissions critically—rather than continue the sterile rehearsal of real and imagined differences.

REFERENCES

BRODER, D. S. (1987) "Press can't leave questions unasked." Eugene [Oregon] Register-Guard (May 13): 11A.

BROWN, L. (1974) The Reluctant Reformation. New York: David McKay.

LEMERT, J. B. and J. MURPHY (1988) "Do readers want mobilizing information in their news?" Mimeo, School of Journalism, University of Oregon.

LEVY, M. R. and J. P. ROBINSON (1986) "The 'huh' factor: untangling TV news." Columbia Journalism Review 25 (July-August): 48-50.

THRIFT, R. R., Jr. (1977) "How chain ownership affects editorial vigor of newspapers." Journalism Quarterly 54 (Summer): 327-331.

NAME INDEX

ABC News, 16, 45
Abbey, Alan, 76, 83n
Accuracy in Media (AIM), 24
Action for Children's Television (ACT), 24, 42
Adams, John, 9
American Assembly, 77
Americans for Democratic Action, 45
Anderson, Thomas E., 58n
Arendt, Hannah, 34
Arterton, Chris, 77, 78, 83n
Ashmore, Harry, 13
Asner, Ed, 55
Associated Press (AP), 80
Atwater, Tony, 101, 102, 106n

Bagdikian, Ben, 62, 82n
Ball-Rokeach, Sandra J., 55, 82n
Baldwin, James, 61
Bayh, Birch, 78
Bettelheim, Bruno, 34
Blanchard, Margaret A., 20n, 21n
Brandt, Don, 15
Breed, Warren, 65, 70, 91, 106n
Broad, William, 43, 58n
Broadcasting, 114
Broder, David, 109, 115
Brown, Jane Delano, 103, 104, 106n
Brown, Lee, 10, 13, 20, 21n, 108, 115
Bureau of Applied Social Research, 35, 36, 37
Bullock, Robert K., 64, 83n
Bush, Chilton R., 64, 83n
Bush, George, 78
Bybee, Carl R., 106n

Carter, Jimmy, 75, 81
CBS News, 45
Chaffee, Steven H., 53, 59n, 84n
Chavez, Cesar, 73
Chicago Daily News, 61, 68, 69

Chicago Journalism Review, 60, 61, 62 65, 83n
Chicago Sun-Times, 60, 68, 69
Chicago Tribune, 60, 68, 69
Christenson, Reo M., 20n, 21n
Clarke, Peter, 23, 33n, 56, 58n
Columbia Journalism Review, 13, 17, 67
Commission on Freedom of the Press, 20n, 21n, 28, 33n, 108
Cook, Roxana H., 59n
Cordtz, Dan, 79
Coser, Lewis, 34, 35, 36, 42n
Crouse, Timothy, 77, 83n
Crown, Henry (Mrs.), 60

Dennis, Everett E., 7, 23, 33n
De Zutter, Henry R., 62, 83n
Diamond, Edwin, 74, 76, 83n
Donohue, George A., 42n
Douglas, Sara, 70, 71, 72, 83n
Drucker, Peter, 34
Dulaney, William L., 62, 83n

Economy Furniture, 72
Edelstein, Alex S., 14, 21n
Editor & Publisher, 12, 114
Elliott, William, 83n
Evans, Susan H., 23, 33n, 56, 58n

Federal Communications Commission, 26, 57, 72, 73
Federal Trade Commission, 67, 68, 69
Fenno, John Ward, 9
"Ferment in the Field" issue of *Journal of Communication,* 26
Fico, Fred, 101, 102, 106n
Fromm, Eric, 34

Gannett Center for Media Studies, 7
Gannett, 86
Gans, Herbert J., 24, 33n, 64

Gerbner, George, 41
Gitlin, Todd, 72
Gordon, Margaret T., 106n
Graber, Doris A., 75, 79, 83n
Gray, Susan H., 105, 106n
Green, Jane, 65, 83n
Greenfield, Jeff, 13
Grube, J. W., 58n
Guback, Thomas, 83n

Hackett, Regina, 59n
Harris, Fred, 78, 79
Hart, Gary, 81, 109, 110
Heath, Linda, 95, 106n
Hill, Sandy, 55
Hirsh, Michael, 67, 68, 69, 83n
Hirsh, Seymour, 62
Hitler, Adolph, 34
Horney, Karen, 34
Hovland, Carl, 39
Hungerford, Steven H., 91, 92, 93, 106n
Hutchins, Robert Maynard, 20n, 28

Ismach, Arnold, 7

Jackson, Jessee, 63
Jefferson, Thomas, 9
Jess, Paul H., 53, 58n
John Birch Society, 45
Jones, William M., 68, 69
Joslyn, Richard, 75, 84n
Journal of Communication, 26
Journalism Quarterly, 37

Katona, George, 34
Kerber, Greg, 7
Kerlinger, Fred N., 47, 58n, 105, 106n
Kerrick, Jean S., 57, 58n
Kline, F. Gerald, 53, 58n
Krieghbaum, Hillier, 67, 83n

Lacy, Stephen, 50, 58n
Larkin, Jerry P., 55, 59n
Lazarsfeld, Paul F., 34, 35, 36, 37, 38, 39, 40, 42n
Lebailly, Robert, 106n
Lemert, James B., 14, 21n, 44, 48, 49, 53, 55, 57, 58n, 59n, 74, 76, 79, 80, 81, 82, 83n, 91, 92, 93, 94, 95, 96, 97, 99, 101, 104, 106n, 107, 111
Lemert, Rosalie M., 7
Levy, Mark R., 50, 59n, 107, 115

Lewin, Kurt, 34
Lichter, Linda S., 33n
Lichter, S. Robert, 22, 33n
Liebling, A. J., 9, 21n
Los Angeles Times, 14, 114
Louisville Courier-Journal, 15

Mann, Leon, 65, 66, 83n
Mann, Thomas, 34
Matusik, David, 50, 58n
McCarthy, Eugene, 81
McClure, Robert D., 76, 79, 83n
McCormick, Edward, 63, 84n
McGovern, George, 65, 76, 81
McWilliams, Robert O., 20n, 21n
Merton, Robert K., 35, 36, 42n
Mills, R. Dean, 17, 18, 21n
Minnesota Press Council, 16
Mitzman, Barry N., 59n
Mogavero, Donald T., 14, 15, 21n
Murdock, Dulcie, 106n
Murphy, John, 111

National Labor Relations Board, 72
National News Council, 16, 17
National Youth Administration, 35, 36
Nessen, Ron, 74, 76, 81, 83n
Nestvold, Karl, 83n
Neumann, Franz, 34
Newark (University of) Research Center, 35, 36
New York Times, 14, 103, 104
Nieman Reports, 17
Nixon, Richard, 76

Oakes, John B., 89, 106n
Olien, Clarice N., 42n
Oukrop, Carol, 94, 106n

Patterson, Thomas, 75, 76, 79, 83n, 84n
Payne, David E., 48, 59n
Payne, Kaye Price, 48, 59n
Pecora, Norma, 83n
Phillips, David P., 48, 59n
Polich, John, 16, 21n
Princeton University Office of Radio Research, 35
Pritchard, David, 62, 63

Quill (magazine of the Society of Professional Journalists), 12

Rada, Stephen E., 72, 73
Rainville, Raymond E., 63, 84n
Rarick, Galen, R., 38, 42n, 83n
Raskin, A. H., 14, 21n
Reader, The (Seattle), 13
Register-Guard, The (Eugene-Springfield, OR), 96
Robinson, John P., 50, 59n, 107, 115
Robinson, Michael J., 75, 84n
Roshco, Bernard, 42n, 104, 106n
Rokeach, Milton, 59n
Rothman, Stanley R., 33n

St. Louis Journalism Review, 13
Sanford, Terry, 78
Santucci, Claramae, 61
Schramm, Wilbur, 35, 42n
Schudson, Michael, 18, 21n
Schwantes, David L., 53, 59n, 101, 104, 106n
Schwengels, Marlyss, 94, 95, 96, 97, 106n
Sears, 67, 68, 69, 70, 91
Seib, Charles, 15
Seither, Michael A., 59n
Shaw, David, 13, 14, 21n
Shriver, Sargeant, 79
Sinclair, Upton, 9, 21n
Stempel, Guido H., III, 41, 42n, 47, 56, 59n
Sussmann, Leila A., 83n
Swales, Luita B., 58n

Tans, Mary Dee, 53
Terkel, Studs, 60, 61, 64, 84n
Thrift, Ralph, Jr., 41, 42n, 87, 88, 89, 90, 99, 106n, 107, 115
Tichenor, Phillip J., 41, 42n
Tillich, Paul, 34
Time Magazine, 16
Times-Mirror, 86
Tuchman, Gaye, 33n, 84n

Udall, Morris, 75
United Press International (UPI), 28
Upholsterer's International Union, 72, 73

Vanderbilt University TV News Archives, 110
Vienna Research Center, 34, 36
Village Voice, The, 13
Von Bismarck, Otto, 9

Wade, Nicholas, 43, 58n
Washington, Betty, 68, 69
Washington Journalism Review, 13, 17, 74
Washington Post, 15, 103, 104, 114
Weardon, Stanley T., 106n
Weaver, David, 25, 33n, 84n
Westley, Bruce H., 47, 59n
Whitney, D. Charles, 26, 33n
Wilhoit, G. Cleveland, 25, 33n, 83n
Wilmington News-Journal, 15

Zhao, X., 84n

SUBJECT INDEX

ABC News, 16, 45

Academic critics of media, 11, 27-28, 38-40

Academics' flight from Hitler, 34

Access to news, inequalities in (see Sources in the news)

Accuracy in Media (AIM), 24

Accuracy of journalists' perceptions of audience interest, 113

Action for Children's Television (ACT), 24, 42

Administrative research, 11, 38-40

Advantages of empirical media critics, 40-42 (see also "Empirical school"

"Afghanistanism" in environmental news, 85, 91-94, 105, 113

Alternative newspapers, impact on mainstream papers, 113

American Assembly, 77

Americans for Democratic Action, 45

Associated Press (AP), 28, 80

Audience interest in mobilizing information, 113-114; perception that news won't have mobilizing information, 113

Audiences for criticism of media, 25-26

Biases in news (see Craft biases, Institutional biases, Political biases)

Broadcasting, 114

Bureau of Applied Social Research, 35-37

CBS News, 45

Chains, effects of on formerly independent newspapers, 85-91, 105

Change in news practices, obstacles to, 13-20, 81-82 (see also Craft biases, Institutional biases)

Chicago Daily News, 61, 68-69

Chicago Journalism Review, 60-62, 65, 83n

Chicago Sun-Times, 60, 68-69

Chicago Tribune, 60, 68-69

Class biases in news, 60-61, 64-65

Columbia Journalism Review, 13, 17, 67

Complaints vs. criticism, 9-11

Conservative biases in news (see Craft biases, Institutional biases, Political biases)

Constants can be ignored in explaining variables, 44-45

Consumer demand and media change, 18-19, 112

Consumer mobilizing information, desire for, 112

Contagion of violence, media role in, 48

Content analysis as research tool, 48

Controlling other variables in research, methods of, 51-52

Convincing journalists to make changes, importance of, 11

Craft biases, 17-18, 22-25, 48-49, 60-61, 64-65, 85, 98-101, 111, 113

Crimes and Detroit newspapers, 48 (see also Contagion)

Critical/cultural studies, 27, 37-40

Criticism vs. critical "one-liners", 9-11, 29-32

Crowd estimates by journalists, 65-66

Cultural/critical studies (see Critical/cultural studies)

Critical research, term preempted by non-empiricists, 38-40

Critical tradition, characteristics of, 10-11, 108-109

Design decisions in empirical criticism, 85-106

Economy Furniture, 72

Editor & Publisher, 12

Editorial policy, and crowd estimates, 65-66

Editorial "vigor," chain ownership and, 85-91, 105

Election campaign coverage deficiencies, institutional causes of, 74-81, 109-110; congressional races, critical study of, 23, 56; presidential primaries (see Presidential primaries)

Empirical research, advantages of, 40-42, 60-84, 108-109; as method of discovering what not in news, 70, 74-75, 77-81, 91-97, 105, 110-111; disadvantages of, 60; false truisms about, 107-108

"Empirical school" of media criticism, 27-40

Environmental "Afghanistanism," 85, 91-94, 105, 110-111, 113

Equalization as method of control, 51

Evaluation research (see Administrative research

Exercises in hypothesis-writing, variable recognition, 58

Experiments as critical tool, controls and precision, 51-52; nontraditional messages and, 49-51

Fair trial—does publicity damage? 52-53

Federal Communications Commission, 26, 57, 72-73

Federal Trade Commission, 67-69

"Ferment in the Field" issue of *Journal of Communication*, 26

Field experiments as critical tool, advantages, 53-54; disadvantages, 54

Field tests as critical tool, network news delay announcement test, 57

Gannett Center for Media Studies, 7

Gannett, 86

"Glass House" syndrome in journalism, 14

Greenfield, Jeff, 13

"Horse-race" coverage of presidential campaigns, 74-77, 79

Hovland, Carl, 39

Hypotheses, 44-47; practice exercises, 58

Hitler, Adolph, 34

Hutchins, Robert Maynard, 20n, 28

In-house criticism, 12, 14, 19

Institutional biases in news, 23-25, 74-81, 94-95, 109-111

Issue coverage, lack of in election coverage, 74-76, 79, 109

John Birch Society, 45

Journal of Communication, 26

Journalism Quarterly, 37

Journalism reviews, 12, 17

Labor in the news, 64, 70-74

Lazarsfeld, Paul F., and the Administrative/Critical research distinction, 34-40, 42n

Liberal bias in news (see Political biases)

Local news, coverage of, 111, 113 (see also "Afghanistanism" Chains)

Los Angeles Times, 14, 114

Louisville Courier-Journal, 15

Marxist school of critics, 27, 29-32, 37-40

Means confused with ends in journalism, 17

Methodology in empirical research, 47-57; combinations of, 55-57

Minnesota Press Council, 16

Mistress or the maid?, 60-61, 64

Mobilizing information, audience interest in, 111-113; crime news and, 111; defined, 48; withholding of, from political news, 48-49, 85, 98-101, 105, 111, 113

Murder-suicides as media "contagion," 48

National Labor Relations Board, 72

National News Council, 16-17

National Youth Administration, 35-36

Newark (University of) Research Center, 35-36

New Hampshire primary, dominance of in news, 74-75, 78, 80-81

News bias (see Craft biases; Institutional biases; Political biases)

News councils, 13, 15, 19

News, doctors and TV, 18-19

Newspapers' unwillingness to cover other news media's flaws, 14, 114

New York Times, 14, 103-104

Nieman Reports, 17

Nonpartisan bias in favor of incumbents, 23, 56

"Objectivity" as a checklist of "safe" procedures, 17-18
Obligations of critics, 11
"Official" source syndrome in news, 17-18, 23-24, 66, 73-74, 85, 101-105
Ombudsman as a source of criticism from "inside", 12, journalists' suspicion of, 15, 19-20; movement, 15, 19-20; reaction to publication of findings, 15, 20
Outside causes of change in journalism, 18-20
"Outsiders" rejected by journalists as unqualified to criticize, 14

Personal reflections by senior journalists, 13
Political bias in the news (see also Election campaign coverage; Institutional biases; Mobilizing information); "nonpartisan" bias favoring incumbents, 23, 56; preopccupation with, 22; favoring incumbents, 23
Political critics, 11
Practice exercises (see Exercises)
Presidential candidates' "personal" lives, 109-110
Presidential primaries, flaws in news about, 74-81
Press councils (see also News councils) 15
Princeton University Office of Radio Research, 35
Professional attitudes of journalists (see Craft biases)
Professional societies as sources of criticism, 12
Publicity, power of, 15-17
Publishers, lack of support for news council idea, 16

Quasi-experiments, 54-55
Quill (magazine of the Society of Professional Journalists), 12

Racial biases, in crime news, 61-63; in news, 61-64, 110-111; in sports telecasts, 63-64, 111
Randomization as last resort, 51-52
Rape coverage—how to improve it, 85, 97-98; problems providing "fair" warning", 94-98, 105

Reader, The (Seattle), 13
Register-Guard, The (Eugene-Springfield, OR), 96
Reporting on the news media, 13, 114
Rewards in journalism, 14

St. Louis Journalism Review, 13
Sears "bait and switch" scandal, 67-70, 91
Social science methodology, 43-59
Social responsibility-oriented critics, 28-33; anecdotal evidence, use in, 29, 60-84; influence in creating shared values for performance, 28-29, 66
"Society" news, class bias in, 64
Sources in the news, 23, 50, 53, 73-74, 78, 80-81, 85, 98-102
Statistics, statistical testing, 105, 114
Study exercises, 58
Subjective bias in news (see Political bias)
Surveys, 49-50; audience, 50; journalists as respondents to, 50; tests of impact of "conventional" messages, 49-50

Technological causes of change in journalism, 18
Television coverage of football (see Racial bias)
Time Magazine, 16
Times-Mirror, 86
Traditions, as obstacles to news changes, 13-20 (see also Institutional biases in news)

United Press International (UPI), 28
Upholsterer's International Union, 72-73

Vanderbilt University TV News Archives, 110
Vienna Research Center, 34, 36
Village Voice, The, 13

Washington Journalism Review, 13, 17, 74
Washington Post, 15, 103, 104, 114
Wilmington News-Journal, 15
"Working class," news about (see Class biases in news; Labor in the news)

Yale studies of attitude change, 39

ABOUT THE AUTHOR

JAMES B. LEMERT is Professor of Journalism at the University of Oregon and author of *Does Mass Communication Change Public Opinion After All?* (1981). More than two dozen of his empirical research articles have been published in such journals as *Public Opinion Quarterly, Journal of Broadcasting & Electronic Communication, Journalism Quarterly, Newspaper Research Journal, Communication Research, Political Communication Review,* and *Journal of Communication.* He was the recipient of two National Science Foundation Fellowships while a graduate student at Michigan State University, and he holds the Ph.D. in communications from that university. He received multiple scholarships and graduated with honors from the University of California at Berkeley. A former newspaper reporter and editor, he has also produced and hosted radio and cable television shows. The courses he has taught at the University of Oregon include public opinion, approaches to criticizing media performance, research methods, reporting, theories of mass communication, mass communication and society, and the craft attitudes of journalists.

NOTES

NOTES

NOTES

NOTES